MAN AND THIS MYSTERIOUS UNIVERSE

---

by

BRYNJOLF BJÖRSET
(SHAMCHER BRYN BEORSE)

THE SHAMCHER ARCHIVES
ALPHA GLYPH PUBLICATIONS

Man and this Mysterious Universe
©1949 Brynjolf Björset (aka Shamcher Bryn Beorse) and © 2015 The Shamcher Archives
Introduction by Carol Sill © 2015

All rights reserved. No part of this book may be reproduced or transmitted in any form or by any means, electronic or mechanical, including photocopying, recording, or by any information storage and retrieval system without express written permission from the publisher. Any unauthorized reprint or use of this material is prohibited.

ISBN: 978-0-9783485-7-1

Library and Archives Canada Cataloguing in Publication

Björset, Brynjolf, 1896-1980, author
    Man and this mysterious universe / by Brynjolf Björset (Shamcher Bryn Beorse). -- The authorized edition.

Reprint, with new Introduction. Originally published: 1949.
ISBN 978-0-9783485-7-1 (paperback)

    1. Civilization--Philosophy. I. Title.

CB19.B53 2015   901   C2015-903258-X

Cover Design: Diane Feught
www.mysterious-universe.shamcher.com

Alpha Glyph Publications Ltd.
Vancouver BC Canada
www.alphaglyph.com

MAN AND THIS MYSTERIOUS UNIVERSE

Contents

Introduction

1. The Trail	3
2. Science	15
3. Art	45
4. Education	55
5. Everyday Life	75
6. the Family of Nations	91
7. Behind Symbols and Dogmas	113
8. A road and a Path	127
9. The Caravan Goes On	135

Acknowledgements & About the Author

Introduction

The book *Man and this Mysterious Universe* was originally described as a synthesis of the many aspects of modern civilization, bringing within its scope the contribution of the East as well as of the West, showing how it has grown from the civilization of the past and how it will probably develop into the civilization of the future. Or as the author put it more simply: a survey of Western and Eastern Sciences.

"Nobody," says Brynjolf Björset, "can claim thorough knowledge in all the fields touched upon in my book. But an overall picture of life is the greatest need of our time. My incurable curiosity forced me to try."

The evolution of humanity and the responsibilities of each of us in this process are described by Beorse in this book which rapidly shifts from one topic to another. However, seen all at once it conveys an image of the totality of the human endeavour: something both outside of time and occurring in time, on schedule, as a great play.

"This comprehensive and refreshing picture is sorely needed at this time of narrow outlook and overspecialization," writes the distinguished psychologist, educator and author, Dr. Philip B. Ballard.

This book was completed before the author had moved to the US and changed his name from Björset to Beorse. Inspired to write by the great sage, Inayat Khan, Beorse combined three former works into one for *Man and This Mysterious Universe*. Written during WWII, then added to with new information, the book was first published in 1949. His previous work, *Distribute or Destroy*, had been in the field of economics. Beorse considerably widened his scope in this next publication, whose title refers to the popular physics book by Sir James Jeans, *This Mysterious Universe*. Here Beorse includes humanity in this assessment of a universe of vibrations and events, creating *Man and This Mysterious Universe*.

In the book, he uses the phrase "the enemy within", which he defines as "anything which prevents man from becoming master of his own destiny".

To readers familiar with Shamcher's work, these contents of this book may be easy to see and understand, but for those who have not yet seen his fully inclusive non-linear approach in action, these few words of introduction may help a new reader to break into the realm in which these ideas find expression. Each chapter takes on a specific topic of human endeavour: Science, Art, Education. But don't be fooled by the seemingly linear approach. Inside each chapter is a shifting mass of variety, much of which may not at first seem to exactly fit that content title. Using examples, personal biographical anecdotes, and stories from others, he moves from the micro to the overview while still keeping the micro-view in place. Also inserted are many references to the work of others, names and articles listed for further review, along with philosophical generalizations. No chapter is complete without a mention of the Creator – not dogmatically but as an embodiment of the unifying energetic field in which all this activity and detailed account has its life and being. For it is ultimately a mystic vision, whatever the topic at hand. In this way a ship and its crew are seen as an embodiment of the finest human prayers.

The Trail outlines the scope of the book, and emphasizes the work on vibration and its measurement by Dr. Brunler as an example of the Western view, while he includes the connection to the great mystic, Inayat Khan as an example of the same wisdom in the East. Giving an overview of the science of vibration, from Paracelsus to James Jeans in Western terms, he connects with the poets of the East such as Rumi and Hafiz, as well as giving an account of his own first meeting with Inayat Khan.

Here Beorse introduces two main themes of the book: the Human Team, and the Only Being.

Science approaches the one world of interwoven vibrations from a variety of angles and disciplines, both Eastern and Western. Again, the human community and love have a place here in the measurement and analysis of conditions and life experience. Looking at rays and vibrations from the point of view of physics, botany, psychology, economics and other scientific fields, in this chapter Beorse brings these forces into focus as a unity, seeing all as efforts "toward the One." Yet he does not deny individual purpose or particular views, and includes in this chapter short anecdotes and examples that illustrate his broad vision of the world of scientific thought, as seen in the mid-20th century.

The chapter *Art* explores the role of artists as humanity's co-creators, with the purpose of bringing humankind forward through a further expression of the impulse of the Creator. Form, sound, vision and the science of vibration are touched upon in this chapter. Beorse envisions a time when artists will contribute to all areas of human life, enriching education, psychology, politics, finance and international relationships.

Education is dedicated to the development of the child, the future of humanity. Through varied anecdotes and accounts, Beorse draws the reader into an ideal of education, one that can prepare the 20th century child for the complexity of the future. One significant component of this is fostering in the child a complete confidence in the inner guidance that comes from awareness of the One Being.

It is in the chapter on *Everyday Life* that all fields of

human activity are shown by Beorse as genuine places of worship. He offers an integrated vision of human life, community endeavours, and society that is nothing less than the manifestation of the divine, in all details and seeming insignificance. Work, war, marriage, divorce, psychology, crime and many other efforts and fields of action are ultimately seen as simply interwoven vibrations. Here is revealed the Oneness of all in the manifestation of any and all. However, these events are also acknowledged as unique and actively evolving circumstances requiring clear involvement. There is no hint of a "spiritual bypass" in this work, but rather a clear assessment and inspired action.

In *The Family of Nations*, Beorse allows his mind to fly shaman-like over the countries of the world, examining preconceived ideas of the various nations and their directions for growth. Once again, details, anecdotes and research findings combine together in synthesis and overview. Beorse exercises great broadness of mind and open awareness in weaving together tremendously diverse forces that were at that time acting upon the world stage, synthesizing them into a cohesive whole that could be viewed in a single glance.

As a great deal of this book was written during wartime while he was active in capacities of spycraft and other aspects of service, the tone Beorse takes in this chapter may seem to no longer apply to the world that we live in today. Some of the details may be of historical interest. However there is a prescience to his approach to assessment of global interaction between nations that is completely applicable to current conditions. This chapter offers a glimpse into the thoughts of the day, and it is possible that insights accounted here may be applied to today's global complexity as well. Following WWII, Beorse saw the Atlantic Pact and the Soviet Bloc as harbingers of an emerging world federation. His broad overview here includes this ideal of federation as a natural phenomenon reflecting the true state of affairs, in which "whatever we do to any nation, to any single man, woman or child, we do it to the Creator or Being who lives and breathes and has his hopes in all."

It is interesting to note that a poem on America by the mystic Irish folklorist Ella Young is quoted here in this chapter. Along with Gavin Arthur (grandson of former US President Chester Arthur) Ella Young was instrumental in the community of Dunites, who lived in the Oceano sand dunes on the California coast. Beorse's later book, *Fairy Tales are True*, features his account of life in the dunes among the free-thinking free-living dunites in this Bohemian Shangri-La. Ella Young gave this community's main cabin its name, Moy Mell, referring to the "pastures of honey" in the afterlife of the Celtic poets and bards.

At the pinnacle of this international overview, great nations interact almost symbolically as if in a vast drama above the globe. After this, Beorse goes behind the scenes into an examination of some esoteric symbols and mystic understandings. *Behind Symbols and Dogmas* offers explanations and examples of some of the more meaningful symbols used the world over down through the ages to refer to the inner path. In this section, Beorse also subtly tackles the tricky subjects of Karma and Reincarnation, basing his analysis on the wisdom approach of the great sage and mystic Inayat Khan, who had been his teacher in the 1920s, and who inspired the writing of this book. Beorse emphasized that life in this world was made for human spiritual awakening and evolution, and "is not to be shunned by him who wants to know and grow." He makes it clear that inspiration and progress are possible even with the responsibilities, wars, worries and jarring influences of this world. He directs modern man to uncover this precious art, offering a resonance of the ancient traditions for contemplation and realization.

Beorse goes further still in *A Road and A Path* to describe in allegory the various ways humanity approaches the ultimate goal. Some go on the main road, others take a steep path. This chapter poetically describes how some seekers may dare to become masterful servants who can bridge Heaven and Earth. Whether on the broad road with all the others, or on the difficult path that is only for one, all humanity takes this same journey. As Beorse expresses the life of the mystic and his approach, he gives clues to understanding this book as a whole: "His urge is to discover the vital elements of Life and make them work, in as many different spheres and activities as he can cover. Based on the knowledge of such vital elements, he gains an insight into all activities at once."

In the final chapter, *The Caravan Goes On,* the book ends with a Sufi teaching story of a masterful servant, before describing of the caravan of Love, that ancient metaphor for the ongoing journey of the soul in the long line of wise companions. Here he even affords the reader a glimpse of the leader of the great caravan, referred to by Sufis as "The Spirit of Guidance."

So what is this book ultimately about? It exposes the mind and thoughts of a contemporary mystic in the middle of World War II and during the immediate post-war recovery. Through creating an ideal to be achieved in each of the topic chapters, Beorse invokes a healing vibration for a shattered world. In the guise of showing an integrated overview of the world situation, it is a revelation of the presence of God in all Life that points the way for seekers to discover this revelation in their own lives.

Carol Sill, Vancouver, BC, 2015

"This book is a synthesis of the many aspects of modern civilization, bringing within its scope the contribution of the East as well as of the West, and showing how it has grown from the civilization of the past and how it will probably develop into the civilization of the future. This comprehensive and refreshing picture is sorely needed at this age of narrow outlook and overspecialization."

Dr. Philip B. Ballard, London, England

To my Wife *without whose inspiration and help this work could not have been completed.*

CHAPTER I

THE TRAIL

Robin can walk, dance, empty ashtrays and play card tricks. With such useful talents, he should also be able to make a living and take care of himself. So what is the difference between him and the rest of us?

Robin is a robot with a ninety-five pound frame filled with switches and wires. He was built by Patrick Rizzo, Detroit automobile factory worker. He was described in the March 1949 issue of *Science Illustrated*. He is the nearest we have to a man-made man.

Dr. Donald H. Menzel of the Harvard College Observatory has spent many recent months listening to cosmic waves translated into sound. "This music of the Spheres," he writes, "was like a combination of gravel falling on the roof and the howling of wolves." In the May, 1949 issue of *Fate*, Mr. Ernst Groth comments on "this new field of exploration. Already man is able to hear sounds from regions of the universe which his telescopes cannot even reach."

This curiosity and the ability to satisfy it mark the difference between man and his robot, for scientific achievements are due, not to individual scientists only, but to the entire community in whose soil they grow. This was brought sharply into focus by Dr. Oscar Brunler when he talked to the Paris-Amsterdam Club in New York, May 1948, about Brain Waves. These were no flippant jokes to Dr. Brunler who had already measured eleven thousand brains! He had delved into that part of man which is beyond the robot.

While listening to the introduction enumerating without

brevity Dr. Brunler's past achievements, my thoughts drifted back. I recalled a day in the Northwestern Australian desert. A caravan wormed its way across the sand dunes. From afar it looked like a huge serpent. As it came nearer, the single camels and their riders could be seen. But they were still one caravan, a living thing with a purpose of its own, different from any single rider and stronger than all of them together. I joined the caravan and became one of the riders. When we neared the coast we changed to trucks. Instead of gentle thuds of camel's hoofs, our music now was the shuffle of deflated tires in the sand. The pace had changed, but the riders were the same. Under the scorching noontime sun or when night fell, headlight beams bursting through the darkness where, before, torches flickered timidly, we weathered the hazards of the journey by keeping close together.

But we quarrelled about the route. Some would follow the main tracks. Others wanted to take a short cut. Others, again, would scorn all tracks and cut a new trail across the desert. The leader of the caravan had to decide. He did not always choose rightly. Neither the trails of the past nor the bold new ideas were infallible guideposts. But over a long period of time, some leaders were proven more successful than others. They were not the ones clinging stubbornly to established trails, nor the ones following recklessly the boldest new ideas, and least of all the tolerant wobblers, wavering between this and that and ending up with a mixture that was neither.

The successful leaders were those large enough to embrace the enthusiasm of the boldest along with the caution of experience, and blend the two in a vision greater than either.

The introduction was over. Dr. Brunler rose, his sharp ascetic face shooting up from his sloping shoulders like a ship's bow penetrating the fog of the unknown. The searchlights from his blue eyes gleamed. His voice was hoarse from thundering against the wall of prejudice.

Man was born, said Dr. Brunler, with certain possibilities peculiar to each individual which would be measured as accurately as the waves from a radio transmitter. There were other, variable radiations, but the key vibrations he called "brain waves" were always the same, unchangeable, for any particular individual. They were the limits and patterns, or the "Fate" within which "free will" might work.

Again my thoughts drifted, though not away from the speaker. Along with his talk about MAN I remembered a recent scientific treatise about the SUN. Years of study by physicists could be condensed and explained in this short treatise because processes known from the tiniest things on earth are also operating in that vast celestial body which, vice-versa, provides clues for our earthly phenomena. Plain, simple principles repeat themselves everywhere, in the smallest cells and in the giants of the spaces; in the materials providing us with cars and gadgets as well as in the tissues of human bodies; in physical "realities" and in our subtlest dreams and thoughts. We like to think of ourselves as free and independent kings as we work or play with due regard to the powers and principles of the universe within which we function. When we don't, we are gently or urgently pushed back on our trail like any erring planet trying boldly to defy the forces we call gravitation, or the rules we call relativity. Man is part of a cosmic caravan.

I had followed its trail in many capacities and places, as sailor, longshoreman, sheep station hand, civil engineer, builder of roads and dams, in the laboratories of science, in newspaper work. I had watched the strong teams and closed shops of nationalities, working with determined Britishers, thrifty Frenchmen, dreaming Turks, singing Russians and sentimental Germans. Tartars, Malays and Maories had taught me the secrets of their tribes. Africans had drummed me into their maddening ecstasy. Australians and New Zealanders had showered on me their hospitality. Learned Chinese and holy Hindus had talked to me of heaven and earth, and South Americans had made me part of their subtle art of living. I had learned to work and play with these teams of limited scope, obeying their rules, mindful of their codes. But in respect to that greater, timeless caravan comprising *humanity*, I was still a wild and untamed steed, shunning captivity, yet curious about its secrets.

Though Dr. Brunler has a queue of letters behind his name, indicating degrees in physics and medicine from Cambridge and the Sorbonne, and a distinguished practice in Harley Street—the Shangri-La of doctors, he is still counted a dark horse of science. Some say he is a jump ahead of his fellow-scientists, while many of the latter doubt that his jumps are in the right direction. He divided the scientific world into batting factions when, in 1926, he predicted the atom could be safely split and the process controlled for industrial purposes.

He came to grips with Albert Einstein, whom he induced to change the first version of the Theory of Relativity. The two are still at grips.

During the fifteen months I have known Dr. Brunler and studied his methods, I have watched the abuse and praise heaped upon him and his brain waves. I have seen him being exposed to acid tests which in all but one case seemed to confirm his theories. His readings cannot be explained away. His *interpretations* are sometimes hard to accept in their entirety. They may bear future adjustment.

Unaffected by discussions or doubts about these details, his general outlook is shared by the group of scientists who made the rediscoveries of vibration and radiation in the twenties the basis of a new and comprehensive explanation of the universe. The most outspoken of these was the British physicist, Dr. James Jeans.

Dr. Brunler, physicist and medical doctor in one, then started measuring radiations from his patients' organs. The very slow thumb radiations of a mentally deficient girl aroused his curiosity. He asked her questions, "Which is your right hand? Left leg?" Such information is stored in one's subconscious mind and can be brought out readily by an intelligent person. Checking with his stopwatch, Dr. Brunler found it took this girl two minutes, eighteen seconds to recover such facts. After a series of measurements he concluded the radiations for thumb and brain of one and the same person were identical. The eleven thousand brains he has studied since then have confirmed his views.

The measurements, he claimed, revealed the mind of a person more accurately than psychological tests. They disclosed a person's attitude toward life, will or lack of will, range of comprehension, mental powers.

After his talk, Dr. Brunler told me about his work with radiation in a different field. Treating fertilizer with fission processes had increase efficiency five hundred times. This "peaceful atom bomb" is already being used in India, where millions have been starving from hunger every year.

Dr. Brunler's face lit up when he talked about his classmate, Dr. James Jeans, whose *Mysterious Universe* was the first proclamation of a universe of radiations and vibrations. It was inspired, to a large extent, by Dr. Brunler.

But who had been the inspiration behind Dr. Brunler? The first one, he said, was Philuppus Aureolus Theophrastus Bombastus von Hohenheim, also called Paracelsus, Swiss-born physician and chemist (1493-1541). Paracelsus opposed nearly every medical theory of his time, introduced sulphur, iron, arsenic, opium and mercury into medical science and finally was thrown out of a window by one of his many professional enemies. According to Dr. Brunler, Paracelsus viewed life and diseases in terms of vibrations or radiations, and his reasons for applying the above-mentioned medicines were their characteristics of radiations in relation to each individual case. If this was the leading theme in Paracelsus' work and practice, it seems to have been overlooked by his followers, and by historians.

A hundred years later, Joseph Saveur, deaf-mute French mathematician (1653-1716), laid the foundation of the science of vibration in musical acoustics (*The History of Music* by Waldo

Selden Pratt). He determined vibration numbers of tones of fixed pitch, encouraged by his contemporary, Louis Carré.

In the nineteenth century, Dr. Von Reichenbach in Vienna rediscovered that the human body sends out radiations, and in the beginning of the twentieth century Dr. Kilner of St. Thomas' Hospital in London made these radiations visible through the "Kilner Screen". Later Dr. Silvans Thompson of Cambridge demonstrated that the radiations from the brain are of a shorter vibration than those of the rest of the body. "Brain waves" are in the violet and ultra-violet range and beyond. Dr. Brunler carried on and measured and interpreted the waves from various known and unknown brains.

I asked, what were these waves? What caused them?

He thought awhile. "The Great Architect," he said. Then he told me about a Hindu friend, the late Inayat Khan, who responded to radiations like a radio receiver to air waves. Inayat Khan had also known James Jeans and seemed to have been one of the inspirations behind *The Mysterious Universe*. To Inayat Khan, said Dr. Brunler, radiation was Life itself. Born and raised in one of those rare families where the genuine treasures of the East are still unpolluted, he was early transplanted to the fertile scientific soil of the West, where he spent the better part of his life.

Inayat Khan had also been a close friend of mine and had influenced me strongly. To my rational western mind imbued with science, he brought treasures of ancient traditions, which I first fought. What I had considered superstitions of the past, he gradually revealed as symbols sparkling with beauty and wisdom.

He made me see that our ideas and achievements are not our own. We are mere exponents of the stream of knowledge handed down through generations and going on through the present into the future. He made me see it so clearly I believed I had always thought so. He made me realize the effect of such an outlook on all aspects of life. By redirecting attention from crippling delusions of individual importance to the Reality of the Human Team, problems dissolve into thin air.

My first meeting with Inayat Khan was in my home town, Oslo. His secretary had asked me to translate some talks to be given by him at our university. I had just returned from his native India, unimpressed by its many fakirs, yogis, teachers, sages. I could not muster too much enthusiasm, either, for the run of native Indians travelling Europe and America under the same pretense. So I eyed my new acquaintance warily. He suffered unflinchingly my scrutinizing glance and, as our friendship deepened, I pondered on my mocking Fate who had let me travel through continents looking in vain for Greatness—finally to find it on my very doorstep when I returned! It appeared Inayat Khan had also met his own best friend practically at his very doorstep after having searched in vain the Himalayas and other glamor spots. Are things worthwhile always close at hand, if one looks for them?

The Inayat Khan I met in Oslo in 1924 was more than the young professor of Indian music who landed in San Francisco in 1910. Then he was an able and patriotic exponent of a fine old tradition. He sang and played the melodies or *ragas* his brothers, cousins and ancestors had dug out of India's past. And he was a teacher of Sufism, a pious and beautiful Eastern tradition that has done much to conciliate warring religious groups in India and has given beauty and art to austere Moslems. The Sufi poets Hafiz, Saadi and possibly Omar Khayam, have graced the name, along with the Turkish musician and philosopher, Jelaluddin Rumi (fourteenth century) who founded the Mevlevi Order of Sufis.

I felt Inayat Khan was greater than this tradition and had a more universal and important message. I often asked him to drop the old name, which, I thought, created a barrier and limited the scope of his appeal. Again, his individual modesty prevailed. His own achievements, his very personality, he said, were not his own, but belonged to the stream of tradition and to him the best of his tradition was embodied in the Sufi name.

Whatever might have been lacking with the old Sufis, he and later generations would add, so the name would be worthy of any cause or message to which it was applied.

Western scholars do not agree on historical Sufism. At present most of them think it originated within Islam, long after Mohammed's death. Inayat Khan, knowing all western sources and others as well, believed Sufism originated in Egypt, long before the known world religions, and that the Hebrew religion, Christianity, Zoroastrianism and Islam all spring from the Sufi tradition, which had to adopt various secret names for fear of persecution. The "Essenes" of the pre-Christian era he considered one of the groups.

Although the publicly available sources on the subject are flimsy, my own studies tend to confirm Inayat's views. He certainly had given more time to this subject than any Western scholar. Inayat Khan's old Sufi teacher, Seyed Madani, told his young pupil on his deathbed:

"Go West to unite East and West through the rhythm of your music, for which task you have been blessed!"

As the years passed, Inayat came to consider the words "East and West" suggestive of more than geographical directions. He understood them as any two sections of humanity divided by disharmony. And the words "the rhythm of your music" also began to have more intrinsic meaning. For the young singer gradually saw or sensed everything in life in terms of rhythm, vibration or music. But the vibrations he perceived were not cold and barren swirls of inanimate matter. They were the compassionate activities of LOVE, the love of the all-pervading Spirit in which we live and Who lives in us and which he called "The Only BEING."

Western science and religion have not always remembered that this Spirit, or GOD, is the ONLY BEING. God has been considered a separate and haughty ruler, punishing or rewarding. This monstrous "God" was rightly debunked by science, but nothing better was put in His place—except by a few sincere men and women of the past to whom "God" was not merely the fierce boss of their sect, whose existence they must believe in or perish. Their God was the undefined ideal toward which all men were moving. Their God was the living reality which this whole universe was approaching, in which every being had its life and existence then and there. The stars and planets, the rocks, trees, plants and that which made them grow: also animals and men and that which made them think, act and want to be honest, kind, heroic—all that and more was their God, which grew with them, surviving changing civilizations and varying degrees of knowledge—a God that could not be lost.

Frightened by the absurdity of battling sects and their fierce punishing "Gods" apart from men, people today turn away from the world picture presented by religion, looking instead to science. When the 200-inch Palomar Telescope was completed in June, 1948, the scientists in charge excelled each other in coy understatements. The little mirror would not do much, merely pose new questions, without giving answers. But earlier, in scientific publications, they had predicted "the little mirror" might enable us to see the limit of this universe and beyond; that the expanse of our world might be measured and new worlds seen; that we might learn whether the universe was becoming smaller or bigger and when and how the end would come; that we might know our Martian or Venusian neighbours, if any. Undaunted by unsuccessful attempts in the past few years, we hope to send a man-made planet into space and have it circle around the earth 600 miles above our heads gathering additional information.

Feeling, perhaps, that Americans were reaching too exclusively for the stars, Russian brethren have been boring beneath the crusty surface of the earth. In the Gora Blagodatnaya mine in the Ural mountains, a Russian engineer locked himself into a mechanical "mole" and proceeded to travel in comparable comfort down through the earth at a pace of thirty feet per hour, his vessel bristling with recording instruments.

The worlds above and below are being conquered. What more could we want to know?

Man.

Medicine knows bits about his body. Psychology makes passes at his mind. But what drives and urges made him and keep him going? How do these fit into vast time and space? Are there a million battling and unrelated forces or is there one cohesive power in which others merge or will merge? If so, may we know it? And what good will it do to know it, or try to know it? Will we do better in business?

Yes, the very effort could not fail to improve efficiency and income, as a general rule, though not at the expense of neighbors and competitors (which seems to add so much pleasure to the achievement), but along with them. Will we become healthier? Less tired? Yes, increasingly, as wisdom acquired in the service of the Caravan will season our hopes of "never to be tired" or "becoming better and better every day in every way." Will international relations improve? As much as they can be improved with greater clarity, and the resulting incitement for the well-intentioned to carry out what they want promptly without waiting for the not-so-well-intentioned. Finally, to those brave eccentrics who yearn to know what life is all about and do things worthwhile, there will be particular satisfaction.

In other words, this is going to be a success story, as all stories are required at this present glamoralistic age. What kind of success story? Money success? Social, professional, progressional, Hollywoodial or just plain phenomenal success? Inayat Khan saw success only in the three words: Love, Harmony, Beauty. Only that which created these three things was success. They were to him the goal of life, or the principle upon which it is patterned. So it appears also to the scientists who now think in terms or radiation or vibration. But our present civilization, its institutions, theories and teachings in individual, national and international matters, is not based on this concept, yet. It is not based on any definite concept.

The vision of radiation begins to do miracles when applied to our behaviour toward friends and acquaintances. This aspect was as important to Inayat Khan as any part of his work as a scientist or artist. A friendship meant to him a lifelong engagement with unending obligations as well as a source of deep satisfaction. Casual acquaintances, owners of hotels where he stayed, bellhops, waiters, delivery boys, glowed under the warmth of his glance, his handshake, his words. Listeners at his concerts would forget the melodies he played or sang for something greater they could not explain. From a purely physical point of view, his voice was not unusual, but its effects were. The words he sang or spoke were like birds winging their way into the listeners' minds and nestling there, living and growing, years after he had passed away. His words to close friends might cause opposition or resentment at first, but the final result was always harmony and beauty because, perhaps, they were inspired by love—the gentle love which is felt between man and woman or between a mother and her child, or the fierce and unyielding love which holds the atom together, keeps the electrons to their curved course and guides the planets on their flights. This is the power which binds men and women into communities and nations of such strength that members may wish to sacrifice even their own lives to secure the continued independent existence of their community. This is the spirit which determined to create this whole universe with its myriads of details and set out to do it, and which keeps it running and evolving.

The clue to knowing and consciously living in this spirit, he would say, is not a particular brand or amount of learning, not mastery of certain philosophies, nor "goodness"—meaning too often a miserly accumulation of barren virtues. What matters is range of perception of mind *and heart* or, in the terminology of physics: range and intensity of vibration. In everyday language, this means people who can respond, who are "very much alive." Their hearts and minds are like running water, fresh and sweet, always covering new ground, while he who allows his thoughts, feelings and habits to freeze to solid ice, limits his own vision and hampers the progress of his community, however "good" he may be. What matters is not who we are, but what we are able to become.

During the invasion of Sicily, one United States ship found itself pinioned in the white shafts of five searchlights from shore. The ship was within easy gunning distance. Ernie Pyle tells us in *Brave Men* about the reaction of one man on board who said, "The fellow standing next to me was breathing so hard I could not hear the anchor go down. Then I realized there wasn't anybody standing next to me."

This, it is said, is how it feels to live in the radiation of Reality. One cannot hear the rattling chains of one's humble self any more than that sailor could hear the anchor chain. This is how I felt on a September day in 1926 when Inayat Khan asked me to write. Eighteen years went by before I started. It took the jolt of a World War to put me in the writing mood. Torn between eagerness and reluctance, I armed myself with notebook and pencil and began jotting down things during London nights while Jerry robots roared; on trucks and ducks while driving along battle-scarred roads or crossing mine-infested rivers of war-torn Europe on the heels of a resourceful enemy; in the burnt and ravaged villages of the Russo-German front beyond the Polar Circle. I wrote and rewrote while a troubled world passed from war to a jittery peace. I gave it a final touch during a trip through Europe in 1949, when battle scars were healing.

Following the trail of the Caravan, I have tried to bring into focus an overall comprehensive picture forming in my mind.

Chapter 2

Science

Once upon a time, when man had stilled his hunger, he began to wonder, and that was the origin of science. He wondered how he could make a better catch next time, and he also wondered with the pure motive of gaining knowledge. He wondered about the fields and forests, the sea and the sky, the beasts and birds, his fellow men, himself. He joined other wonderers and they wondered together in groups, choosing as teachers those who could give the best answers to their questions.

Some of these groups accepted certain philosophies of life and developed into scientific "schools" or religious traditions. Others kept alive the spirit of research, rejecting dogmas. The latter were the forerunners of modern science.

But what is modern science? A kindly wizard, providing us with gadgets? Yes, but now we want to know the depth of his mind and his secret yearnings. We may think this impossible, awed by his knowledge which reaches from the tiniest electron to the entire universe. But every single item in the world of science was brought there by some human mind, and can therefore be retraced by human minds. Remembering this, and promising nothing, we can begin at the beginning and see where we land.

Science was early divided into groups, according to the direction of man's wondering. He looked upon matter and created the sciences of physics and chemistry. He saw great parts of the earth at once, and this was geography and geology, but when he lifted his eyes to the stars, there was astronomy.

He created mathematics as a tool of his thoughts. He looked at living things and developed the sciences of biology, botany and zoology. The next step on the ladder of the living, he realized, with embarrassment perhaps, would be himself. He looked at his body and reshaped the old science of medicine along experimental lines. He looked at his thoughts and called them psychology. He saw himself in relation to his fellow men and there was sociology, branching out into economics, political science and international relationships, languages. Stretched out in time, all this became the science of history.

Continuous division and subdivision of Science has been necessary in gaining detailed knowledge, but equally important was the urge for a synthesis, a desire to see the whole picture, of science and of life. The many details could not be correctly seen and shown in right proportions without an overall picture.

The science of physics first provided such a picture. In the late twenties some prominent theorist physicists evolved the hypothesis of *vibration* as an explanation of the atom and of the universe. The principle of vibration had been well known for a long time. A violin string vibrates when it is struck, causing the air to vibrate, which again causes our ear drums to vibrate and so forth. The new idea was that everything was vibration, even the atoms of the violin string, and the electrons of the atoms, and also human tissue and even human thoughts and emotions and aspirations. The latter notion drew spiteful comment from the opposition. Dr. James Jeans and others were called "mystics"—until research physicists supported the theory by experiments. As a result, even the nickname "mystic" was considered almost respectable.

The hypothesis of vibration has no room for any indivisible "particle" in this whole universe. All we perceive with our senses or by means of instruments are merely sets or systems of vibrations in a uniform substance matter or "no matter at all" if we can think in such a term. Stars and planets, minerals, plants, animals, men, thoughts, emotions, even neutrons and electrons, the smallest items known so far, all these are just so many different forms of vibrations within vibrations. In other words, matter and life are nothing but rhythmic movement. This points right to the nebulous term "the fourth dimension". The three dimensions are the three extensions of any body in space, called, for example, length, width and height. The fourth dimension is the time factor, the rhythm or vibration making time and space an interrelated entity. The "splitting of the atom" is a disturbance of the rhythmic movement within an atom so that certain systems of vibrations called electrons and neutrons are hurled out of the atom system like planets being hurled out of a solar system. Part of the energy bound within an atom is released and made to work outside. Despite an impressive amount of supporting research, the theory of vibration is still a hypothesis, which means it is not yet *generally* accepted as law. Some spend their days trying to disprove it. But argumentation may not solve the riddle. Its mystery will only yield to experience, gained through trial and error. When Isaac Newton's scientific hypothesis of gravitation was accepted, temporarily, this enabled later scientists to discover its flaws and evolve more complete and comprehensive explanations, including the Theory of Relativity. Similarly, no decisive conclusion can be reached about the world picture in the light of vibration except by trying it out and living it. This is what we are doing throughout these pages. Our achievements and ideas, joys and sorrows as individuals, family members and citizens are viewed in the light of vibration. Only in this way can the meaning of radiation and vibration be realized, and the "theory" appreciated. To those who already are convinced of the vibration world picture, the book may be considered a humble contribution toward the joint mastery of our destiny.

Why are some convinced, while others are still doubting? Are the "believers" just too credulous? Not necessarily. They may have collected facts which the doubters have ignored. Also, there are great differences in human perception. Inventors, scientists and artists often reached their objectives through glimpses of perception that only later were supported by facts and a logical build-up. And sometimes great discoveries were not equal to his inventive genius. Similarly, mediocre or untrue results were accepted because of the ability with which they were expounded and defended.

In the Western world, the theory of vibration was first set forth by Paracelsus (1493-1541) according to Dr. Oscar Brunler of Cambridge and the Sorbonne. Long before that, it was part of the world picture of philosophers and teachers of Greece, Persia, Egypt, India. It has been perpetrated by writers and poets such as Pythagoras in Greece, Hafiz, Saadi, Rumi in Persia and Turkey, Krishna, Shankaracharia in India, the four Evangelists. The allegorical references of many religious scriptures to life as an "ocean" (of waves) appears to spring from this conception of vibration, and so does the picturesque tale about "stilling the storm," meaning to still or harmonize violent emotional vibrations in oneself or others. The scientific discoveries and theories that, from 1926 on, revived this old world picture have given new meaning and dignity to old traditions.

In the light of vibration, "living" or "dead" things, "spirit" or "matter," cease to have distinctive or definite meanings, all things dissolving into One Indivisible and Living Being. Like the rhythmic waves from a radio transmitter, so do all things and beings within this one Being send out their messages. There is no great difference between rock, a tree, a man or a loving thought carving its way through the universe like a ray of the sun.

We register these messages by means of our known senses, sight, hearing, smell, taste, feeling, mental or emotional facilities. In addition, some claim to sense thoughts or emotions directly, without the medium of hearing or seeing. Present reaction to such claims are mainly scornful rejection or blind acceptance—both equally unprofitable. Fakers and cranks apart, sensory perceptions beyond what is generally accepted are frequent. But the interpretations are often premature. Spiritualistic mediums, for example, have sometimes amazed audiences by relating incidents the mediums couldn't possibly know from ordinary sources. The incidents may have been known only to one person present and a departed friend of this person. The popular and wishful explanation is "communication with the dead." An understanding of vibration would have provided a number of possible explanations of which messages from the dead would be the most remote, telepathy the most probable (if fakery had been eliminated) *even if the person present had forgotten the incident.*

A scientist's views on telepathy are found, for example, in *The Reach of the Mind,* (William Sloane, 1948) by J.B. Rhine of Duke University, Durham, N.C. His book was briefly reviewed by John J. O'Neill in the *New York Herald Tribune* and *Your Mind,* June, 1948. Dr. Rhine has investigated telepathy, clairvoyance and other extra-sensory perceptions. He has seen signals and messages transferred directly between minds thousands of miles apart. But the receiving minds in his experiments have not yet been sure the signals were correct or in right sequence. The connections between conscious and subconscious realms of the mind have not been clearly established. He feels this will be accomplished in the near future. The receiver of telepathic messages will then know if a signal is right. Dr. Rhine thinks telepathy may be developed to such perfection that war plans or criminal plots will be detected the moment the plotters start thinking. War and crime would then become impossible.

Individuals who in the past have been able to establish the connection between the conscious and subconscious realms of the mind and who were sure of telepathic messages, have been too few to warrant scientific laws or conclusions.

In terms of physical science, telepathy means that receiving minds register vibrations emitted by sending messages. Vibrations from incidents that may have been forgotten still go on in the subconscious mind. This is why a sensitive receiving mind, such as a spiritualistic medium, may pick up such forgotten stories. But often they get mixed up with vibrations from other sources. When the medium presents the resulting concoction, the credulous clients will be heartbroken pondering upon the feebleness of mind their dear ones seem to have acquired after passing away. Communication with the "dead" may be within the scope of some men, but premature conclusions benefit nobody. The same applies to all extra-sensory perceptions, the contents of which are often found to be inferior to friendly advice picked up by our plain everyday ears.

Along with the scientists of the West, Yogis and Mystics of the East have studied and practiced these arts. There are lightweights and fakers in the West and perhaps to an even greater extent in the East. But, as the saying goes, "counterfeit coins prove that real coins do exist." There are real Mystics and Yogis who do not spend their time on beds of nails any more than Dr. Vannevar Bush. With the light shed on these matters by Dr. Joseph B. Rhine and other psychologists, and also by other branches of Western science, we can no more scoff at the stories of Yogis reading the secrets of any mind thousands of miles away. Whether true or not, such feats now seem within the range of the possible. Even the "mantramistic sciences" now make sense. By uttering certain words or sounds (mantrams) Yogis were supposed to heal or kill or change the minds of men or even tear down houses! For centuries, such tales merely provided us with ideas for horror fiction or for exploitation of the credulous. Today we are forced to look seriously even upon this class of Yogi.

Technically their "mantramistic sciences" have been confirmed in principle. In *Science Illustrated,* May 1947, Mr. John E. Gibson reports old cases and recent experiments in which the vibration of sound was killing or driving off insects, birds, animals; cracking or tearing down houses; scattering the powers of a brain; undoing the sense of balance of a human system. A foghorn nearly killed a man who was too near when it burped. A "sound gun" under construction was considered likely to kill enemy soldiers at two hundred feet or disable them at a quarter mile.

The physicians were not alone with their vibration theory. Outstanding representatives of medical science have viewed patients and diseases in terms of radiation or vibration, beginning with Paracelsus in the sixteenth century (if Dr. Oscar Brunler is right) on down to Dr. Von Reichenback of Vienna, Dr. Kilner at St. Thomas' Hospital in London in the nineteenth century and Dr. Silvanus Thompson and Dr. Oscar Brunler of Cambridge in the twentieth century. Dr. Brunler, particularly, based diagnosis as well as cure on the measurements of radiation or vibration. Dr. Phil. Emil Rasmussen of Copenhagen, Denmark, originally a botanist, has evolved a diagnosis and cure of early cancer based on radiation. Dr. Med. Ivan Tisell and Dr. Signe Danielson of Stockholm, Sweden recommend and employ his methods.

Botany was examined and explained in the light of vibration by Dr. Chandra Bose, Hindu botanist (not to be confused with Mr. Chandra Bose of political fame.) Dr. Bose discovered that the cells of trees and plants reacted differently to different people or animals approaching them. In some instances, leaves and flowers opened measurably to certain persons and closed when other persons came near. It looked as if the trees and leaves and flowers felt attraction or repulsion toward human beings and animals. The trees liked some and disliked others, according to the harmony or disharmony of the vibrations of the approaching beings related to their own. If Dr. Bose's explanation is correct, one may say that he has shown us how trees and plants reach up into the worlds of animals and men. It is another demonstration of the unity of life.

In the animal kingdom some of the first experiments were carried out with our friend, the dog. The research brought out a definite language between dogs and other animals as well as between dog and man. Different kinds of barks and growls—some say inaudible sounds as well—convey suggestions such as: come, go away, stay where you are, I warn you, I like you, I would like to come but I dare not. Dogs can express sympathy, enthusiasm, loyalty, sorrow and joy. In the African campaign, some soldiers of British Eighth Army watched a dog's reaction to human language—and bombers. They called him "Jerry" for he was found in an air raid shelter in a town they had just captured from the Germans. They tried to speak to him, but it was evident he did not understand English. Then one soldier spoke some German words. The dog pricked up its ears and listened but with an expression of pained surprise: there was something wrong with the Limey's German accent! However, in the course of a few days the dog picked up the English words and became a perfect Cockney. Now British planes appeared, and the dog tried to run to the shelter and seemed surprised when no bombs were dropped. A little later German planes came. Now the dog remained perfectly calm and was most upset when the German planes dropped bombs! The explanation seemed to be that while he was with the Germans he had learned to distinguish the noise of the British planes and feared them, for they always dropped bombs on the German positions while, naturally, German planes did not. Now, with the town in British possession, it was the other way around and it did not take Jerry long to find out. How? Evidently not by pondering deeply upon international relations, but simply by reflection. The thoughts and fears of the soldiers seemed to be reflected in Jerry's mirror mind, which caught and repeated the vibrations of the soldiers' emotions. This, also, seems to be the process by which many domestic pets "read" their masters' minds, often more correctly than human friends can. The animal's mind is simpler, more one-pointed and concentrated, more exclusively focused on its master.

The emotional relation of wild animals to man is usually very different. In many cases it is strong repulsion. Most lions scrupulously avoid man when not challenged to fight. They see in him the most formidable obstacle to their kingly reign and their hatred for him seems to be different from all their other emotions, and more persistent. Some birds appear to consider it a calamity to be touched by a human hand. They have been observed to attack and kill a fellow bird who has been thus disgraced.

Like domestic animals, so also wild beasts and birds have been found to communicate with each other by languages all their own, often involving sounds too coarse or too fine for human ears to hear. Such languages, along with silent emotional relationships of love or hate, are sinews of our world of interwoven vibrations, embracing and connecting living and so-called dead things. It is manifest in the circling of electrons around the core of the atom, and science may also some day find vibrations of an even tinier order within the electron, and within the positrons and neutrons in the core of the atom. It is also manifest in the giant movements of the planets around the sun, and of other planets around other suns, and in the movements of the suns among themselves.

In the middle of this multifarious system of vibrations stands man, who is part of it, but who also is able to understand and appreciate in increasing measure the whole drama.

Understand—yes, but only as a timid spectator?

With the budding of knowledge the prominent sensation is wonder. But as insight deepens, he becomes increasingly interested in the success of the great game. He wants to take part, and gradually he burns with a flaming desire to cooperate. With the ardor of a boy who begins to understand the craftsmanship of his father, he joins in the Creator's work. He becomes a collaborator rather than an onlooker and worshipper. His thoughts and desires gradually merge into those of the creator. This, say the sages, is the real "Heaven" or "Nirvana"—the active participation in the creation of the universe, a far cry from the vague dreamworld usually connected with these two words.

Man lives by vibrations. There are the seats of his physical senses, eyes, ears, nose, tongue and the centres of feeling, each of them tuned to the particular kind of vibrations which feed them and give them worry or delight. Food brings into the body vibrations which sustain and quicken the vibrations of tissue, blood, brain matter and nervous system—or break them down if this food is not suited to this particular individual. The vibrations of fluids are lighter, quicker, and more penetrating than those of most solid foods, and the vibrations of air, gasses, smoke, taken in with breath, are quicker and more penetrating than those of most fluids. There are the subtler vibrations of sound and color which also influence physical tissue as well as thoughts and emotions.

For perhaps half a million years man has been exposed to and accepted these influences as a matter of course. Exquisite curls and beautiful patterns of vibrations have been churning around in and about him without as much as a nod of recognition on his part. But a few thousand years ago he became curious and just recently learned to measure the heat energy of the food he ate, calling the measuring unit a "calorie." He thought he had found the entire secret of food values and a few tried to arrange their diet accordingly—with sad results. There were important things he had overlooked, some of which he later embodied in the sciences of minerals and "vitamins," the latter meaning simply living or life-giving items. This was cleverly put, for if he found there was still something lacking after the known vitamins had been supplied, he would just go in search of another and new vitamin. The most recent one is "K", but who can believe this will be the last? Present research, particularly regarding the effect of food on thoughts and emotions, may lead to a more basic scientific principle than that of scattered vitamins and salts. The tragedy of malnutrition during World War II, for example, had its bright side in offering opportunities for research on an unprecedented scale, with humans as guinea pigs. Large groups of people lacked certain kinds of vitamins or minerals for long periods. This changed mental faculties and emotional trends. The effects of thoughts and feelings upon physical conditions, on the other hand, has been extensively studied after the war. This is called Psychosomatic Medicine. Even *teeth* can be hurt by emotions. See, for example, Madelyn Davidson's article in *Your Life,* June, 1948. These findings may be both simplified and amplified when calories, vitamins and mineral salts can be specified in terms of vibration. Also thoughts and feelings can be so specified, thus a comprehensive and inclusive science of vibration may emerge, like the solution of a crossword puzzle, to supercede and replace the brave but embryonic theories of calories and vitamins.

Upon such clarification of medical science, we would be able to choose all influences from outside so that life within and without could be experienced and enjoyed with maximum completeness. What about our span of years? Would it be increased? The happiest and most well-balanced persons throughout history have had no particular wish to cling to life beyond their period of maximum health. This may become the general attitude when mental and physical health will be the normal condition for the majority. Men will pass on without regret, being missed but not mourned. As distinguished Dr. Harry Benjamin once put it, "Our goal should be not to add years to life, but add life to years!" Besides, the science of vibration may some day confirm that there is a continuation.

The science of vibration may cause changes in eating, drinking, and smoking habits along with a growing tendency toward greater individual choice. This very thought may give the jitters to housewives and manufacturers of foods, beer, liquor, tobacco. But, says an old phrase, of all animals the human is the slowest in changing habits. As everybody knows, this is pure nonsense. He happens to be the fastest, otherwise how could he be the only one having developed the atom bomb? Nevertheless, he is slow enough to calm down any manufacturer beset with reconversion headaches. It takes time to change a rhythm or vibration of habit. Long after the last pieces of the old machinery will have uttered their final old-age squeak, there will still be millions howling and clamouring for "that prewar product" however hairy it might be compared to later developments. Besides, along with the science of vibration will come an avalanche of new inventions, improvements, new uses for old materials. The result will be an unprecedented increase in wealth. Everybody will be so much better off that it will be simply a financial necessity and a relief from taxation to develop new products and build new plants.

There are already many signs of such coming changes. Research in American hospitals and laboratories have for example brought out hitherto unknown health-promoting qualities in goats' milk, rabbit meat and other foods that have so far been sparsely produced. But if such research is going to change the eating habits at all, it will take such a long time that food producers will have no difficulty in adjusting, gradually, their stock and equipment to meet the changing demands. Similarly, the more spectacular changes to be expected from the application of the science of vibration will also be stretched over such a long period of time that no inconvenience will be felt by alert producers. The same applies to manufacturers of tobacco and cigarettes. There is an urge at present for new and better products that would give a real lift without repercussions or discomfort to the smoker and his surroundings. The kings of our smokes will have ample time to provide such products before demands become too bumptious, and they will still retain ample markets for the "good old stuff" as long as anything or anybody is left of the old production outfits.

The new challenge to manufacturers of tobacco and liquors stems partly from the war. For missions involving danger or exposure, all the armed services issued preparations and stimulants that were not only highly nutritious but also had plenty of kick and glory—without hangovers or smoky eyes. In addition, there were inventions not yet exploited, for example, negative ionization of air which, when inhaled, makes one see all the castles and fair maidens associated with proper doses of smoke-infested alcohol—but none of the pink elephants. This is the beginning of a trend that the science of vibration may complete.

Smoking has been considered a token of peace and

friendship, even from the time of the red Indians who came together for a smoke to settle differences after a good fight. Smoking was a symbol of peace restored. Similarly, in modern civilization the act of offering another a cigar or cigarette is a gesture of friendship, a generous coming forward to meet the other fellow. The cigarette a soldier offers to a prisoner of war, or to a spy who is going to be shot, is a token of friendship and respect for a fellow soldier and human being even if he be an enemy, nay, even if he be a spy! The quality of smoke, therefore, is naturally going to improve as man advances until it will become a real treat to everybody, safely enjoyable for the frail as well as the hearty, for children and teenagers as well as adults.

Our drinks form another bond of social relationship. They cause a happy and friendly state of mind comparable to the compassion experienced by religious devotees. In ancient traditions, wine was therefore used as a symbol of love and ecstasy and, being a love-hungry and friendly creature, man proceeded to increase both the strength and quantity of his doses, while paying little heed to quality and lasting enjoyment. To his dismay he experienced a break-down of self-control and judgement during his short spells of enjoyment and, what was worse, a gradual degeneration and a lulling of the brain cells to crude apathy—if the practice were persisted in! Some got a splitting headache as a sound warning. Others were not so fortunate. They got no headaches themselves—only gave them to others!

No doubt the Fords, the Kaisers and the Mayos of the brewery business, the distilleries and the public recreation service must now be working overtime so they soon can offer the real thing to weary workers who come home after dull routine jobs, to seamen arriving in port with high hopes and to our young manhood—and womanhood—in colleges and universities, who would like so much to admire their elders and the great, big world they are going to take over.

Someday, maybe, men will know how to pursue these

exalted states of mind without physical means, by purely mental or emotional processes, which some ancients claimed to do and which they called, in their flowery language, "to tune one's vibrations to the music of the spaces." In these processes breath was said to play a great part although that was not the only way. Breath, according to these ancients, is not only an inhalation of fresh air and an exhalation of foul air. Breath may be called the very vibration which links the personality of an individual with the world around him. Not only his lungs, but every atom of his body, mind, and spirit breathes rhythmically and through this breathing, absorbs the life of the universe. Controlling the breathing in the lungs gradually extends control to all units of the personality. After total breathing has been brought somewhat under control, a thought or emotion may be linked to it and this will, as it were, swing the thought into the rhythm of one's system and make it a part of one's personality. Saints of old, for instance, at each inhalation contemplated "This is not my body," and at each exhalation "It is the temple of God—who is all and everywhere." That built into their system the thought that their bodies were not themselves but instruments for the Spirit, which is God. In the same way they impressed upon themselves the fact that their thoughts and emotions were also just instruments to be used by the Spirit—God. Consequently, they could no more think or act like selfish adventurers. They began to feel like exponents of the creative Life Eternal.

The breath is also a man's link with other individuals. The audible part of this system of communication—which is not the only part—forms the science of languages, which, in the form of sounds, words, sentences, are conveyed by vibrations of sound to the vibratory system of another being, through his ears. Language, again, is part of the broader science of sociology, man's relation to his family, his neighbours, his community, nation and to humanity, the past tense of which is the science of history.

Language is not merely part of the sciences of sociology

and history, but a cornerstone. It is a peculiar cornerstone in that we know nothing about its origin. If man wanted to learn the art of humility, he could acquire it by contemplating the riddle of language. Until some fifteen years ago, modern languages were believed to have developed from some dull cave man's one-syllable outbursts, prompted by emotions or everyday chores (the "pooh-pooh" and "pow-wow" theory.) But such outbursts were found to have no relation to the patterns of either old or modern language. Besides, new excavations disclosed that many ancient languages were richer, more colourful and more musical than modern ones. This practically did away with Charles Darwin's theory that man has evolved from the ape. A new language theory developed, according to which the ancients emitted musical notes formed into words and sentences. But who were these musical geniuses and where did it all begin? The new "ding-dong" theory does not bring us a step nearer the solution of the riddle, except if we think of Life as a graceful, artistic and scientific vibration of love, instilling in the minds and hearts that can respond, words, sounds, music, language originating beyond the physical world we know.

The present scientific drive to solve the language riddle may well change our entire world picture in the bargain. For a short review of recent research, see for example Morton M. Hunt's article in *Science Illustrated,* July, 1948.

The urge for a closer international cooperation and unity has expressed itself in a number of proposals for a new universal language, but modern research has confirmed the old idea that a language is a living thing indeed. So probably an established, living language will be the universal tongue, or a simplified version of it. At the same time, the many individual languages will be retained with all their traditions, their charm and beauty.

With the development from the poetical speech afire to the modern matter-of-fact languages, words have come to be considered true and exact representatives of thoughts and things, even identical with them. It has been forgotten that words can never be more than vague suggestions. Men have worried, quarrelled and gone to war over words, which, they discovered later, have been interpreted differently, or had had no clearly defined meaning at all. Several modern educational and philosophical societies and groups have taken upon themselves to remind men of the limitations and real nature of words. As words are suggestive of thoughts, but not actually representative of them, a word can never convey the intended meaning unless it is embraced by a mind in a spirit of sympathy and generosity. Discussions in which one person hopes to get the better of the other, and in which "proofs" are offered or demanded, can at best be a good pastime and a training of the mind, but hardly a source of real knowledge or clarity.

People have worried themselves to death or gone out of their minds over words like "eternal," "damned," "devil," "life," "death," "sex," and "saved," "sin" and "virtue," "coward" or "hero"—while the mere understanding of the origin, the vagueness and the limitations of such words would have swept away the worry and made the former sufferer laugh at himself and the ghosts he had harboured in his mind.

College students in American universities have shown a marked improvement in performance after having gone through special courses during which these facts were explained and discussed. Drunkards have become permanently sober and crazy minds have become sane.

An exponent of an organization embracing, among other things, the above point of view, upon being asked what it was all about, replied, "Unmonkeying the world!" Someone asked, "Did you say world or word?" "I might have said both," was the answer.

In ancient India and Greece, Buddha and Krishna, Plato and Pythagoras also taught men the distinction between words and thoughts, the limitations of the human mind. An old monk asked Buddha, in order to test him, "Is the world eternal?"

Buddha's answer was, "With what are you measuring?"

The legends of the Bible are beautiful illustrations of the suggestive nature of words, as opposed to the idea that words are solid and concrete things to quarrel about.

Many modern crusaders defeat their own purpose by discarding the past, believing they have something new. On the other hand, studying the old books in the light of the rediscovered truth will replenish our treasury, open doors rather than close them, unite the present with the past. Thus may be revealed that current of Life which is running through both past and present. This is the current of vibration or love. It is the basis and substance of any human community.

There is an interwoven network of such human communities. The simplest is the family, which originates with the love between two human beings. At the risk of being called unromantic, we may define this love as two individual systems of vibration tuned to mutual harmony and gradually interwoven into a dual accord, maturing into ecstasy. This may happen simultaneously in the soul, mind, heart and body. Then we have the perfect love which poets call "heaven-sent." But this is very rare. Mostly the harmony is near perfect in one sphere only, while in the others there are sighs of resignation or pious hopes. Even in the rose-painted realms of love, there are limitations and compromises. Those who cannot or will not admit this will often spend their lives in wild goose chasing, "looking for a lamb with five legs," as the Swiss say.

But those who bravely join even if love is not complete at first, may have the satisfaction of gradually growing into a perfect relationship. Many modern schools and courses in matrimony overlook this, and set up requirements which, if adhered to, would practically stop marriage. The commendable purpose of this stringency is to lower the divorce rate, but the latter should not be a cause of worry. It is a transitory phase of modern civilization on its road from hypocrisy to honesty. If a marriage after a fair trial does not work and has to be brought to an end, this is no "failure" but one of the indispensable and priceless experiences that become stepping stones of progress. The only loss is the uncalled-for self-reproach or self-pity accompanying such incidents.

Not only a family but any human community or organization derives its strength from some form of love and is based on nothing else. Love of common interests is behind a trade union, an employers' organization. In the community of a city, county, state or nation, there is in addition the love of common soil, ideals and characteristics. There are always hundreds of good reasons for the members of any community to drift apart and start a fight. The only power that may be strong enough to counter and overcome the instinct of separation is love.

Similarly, as long as this power of love is limited in space or kind or number, separation manifests above or beyond these limits. If the citizens of a nation are very patriotic but do not care a bit about citizens of other nations, something unpleasant is bound to happen periodically. Appeals to "tolerance" or "common sense" or "self-interest" in the name of peace can at best only temporarily stave off that war which is an expression of nothing but lack of love. But the moment love, as an emotion, a passion, be extended beyond the nation, *even if only from one side,* this means the beginning of the solution. In the first place, love draws to itself *knowledge* of "the beloved," of the other people from whom trouble may be coming. The lover will know what is brewing and take precautions and proper action, including keeping his powder dry, but also aiding when this is needed.

If "love" be considered a too solemn term, there is the more modern and picturesque supposition of having "ants in the pants"—an expression which sometimes may be uncomplimentary, but which also has its generous and well-intentioned interpretation. In this interpretation, the "ants" are the irresistible prompting of what some call love, which may not exclude mistakes or exaggerations but will enable the ant-ridden one to make good use even of his mistakes for promoting the progress and well-being of himself and his community. By a frank exchange of information, viewpoints, failures and successes, causes of brewing conflict may be removed or, if the sincerity was chiefly on one side only, the vigilance of the ants would keep one prepared to meet any emergency, sweeping away all indifference, laziness, fear, rendering individuals and the nation as alert, powerful and strong as the physical resources will at all times permit.

If any one should feel that these suggestions are rather too commonplace to be mentioned, he may recall that only a few years ago the international situation was permitted to drift into a World War that certainly could have been nipped in the bud and averted if only one side had known and exercised the vigilance and determination that spring from genuine love. Gestapo sleuths would not have left a trail of crippled patriots if American and British hearts had been awake and in good health.

This thing called love is what holds together the powerful and frequently diverging vibrations of any unit or combination of units. Where it is lacking, divisions into warring sections start. This may be observed in all fields of human endeavour, even in the glorified sanctum of science! The division of science into groups and sub-groups had the commendable purpose of enabling us to master the increasing flood of details. Many a guardian of such tedious details maintained a wide view. Probing the depth of their tiny section of truth, they discovered the pattern of The One. But an increasing number did not see beyond their particular position and went to war against occupants of other positions. Being kings of tiny islands loomed greater in their fancy than being unnamed members of research teams. Love was lacking, the love that feels the pulse of things and makes one humble. In colleges and universities, cold and barren criticism frequently replaced the drive of enthusiasm. Humanity was being eroded by "humanities," branches of science dissolved into marauding bands living off the fat of cultivated lands rather than battling their way into the dense jungles of the unknown. Historians demonstrated little but the old saying that historians repeat themselves (while history does not.) Merely a few of them realized that to keep up with the past would require rewriting the entire human history every tenth year at least. Economists spent their twentieth century's industrial and atomic age quoting and misquoting prophets of the eighteenth century. "Sex analysts" nipped at the fringes of emotional outgrowths and made bold passes at our minds.

Unnoticed by these, the "natural sciences" were making history. The Caravan of Love was rediscovered in the atom and in cosmic rays. The latter have been artificially reproduced, at about one-billionth of the original strength, meaning 300 million electron volts, equal to two thousand 50-kilowatt radio transmitters, in the new Synchrotron at the Massachusetts Institute of Technology. Thus we break into atoms surrounding us and discover their tremendous display of the force of Love. This has revolutionized the sciences of physics, astronomy, chemistry, biology, medicine, veering shyly toward philosophy and religion. It has affected practical psychology in such establishments as The American Institute of Family Relations in Los Angeles. Here "sex" is viewed again in the light and warmth of love and family, while recent schools had torn it loose from the main body of emotions, which is love. "Sex" had been permitted to drift like a lone and dominating monster on the sea of life, an object of shrewd speculations and dark exploitation, a "problem" to which "solutions" were sought. Again it is being realized that there is no solution to such "problems" separately, but reinstated in their proper setting, they change from riddles to blazing powers of progress.

Where does Dr. Alfred C. Kinsey's much-publicized report on The Sex Life of American Men stand in this picture? The cautious may reserve judgement until the work has been completed. It is part of a typical American trend which started some thirty years ago and may be termed "statistical psychology." It seems gradually to replace the stiffer and more dogmatic Freudian approach. With a distaste for public criticism which is typical of the American scene, there has been practically no voice raised against the publication but in some quarters there has been silence. Privately, the many possibilities of error in the short interviews forming the basis of the report have been stressed. *The New Yorker* and others have replied to these unpublished objections that the interviews lasted for hours and were so arranged that mistakes would be checked. This is interesting, but not reassuring. Every lawyer knows the tragic limitations of man as a witness to acts committed either by himself or others. Also, most people are greater dramatists than scientists and love to picture themselves as sexual giants, having indulged in forbidden fruit. Others are prompted by the very opposite urge.

Even counting the mistakes, there is undoubtedly some value for the future in knowing the past, but often this value is over-estimated. *Ideals*, having lived in human minds throughout ages, are no less real than past acts. They are substantial vibrations and, insofar as we make the reality of the future, they are even more important than the past. What Mr. Smith did with his sex life yesterday may be of interest to the curious. I am more concerned with my own sex life tomorrow. It will not be what Mr. Smith did. It may not even be very much influenced with what Mr. Smith did, whatever the men with their noses on the statistical grindstone may think. I am glad to hear about their statistics, but I beg to draw my own conclusions and choose my own emphasis, on the strength of vibrations within myself which may be made to speak louder than statistics about others.

Good (and bad) old Sigmund Freud also tried to see an overall picture and there are elements of love in his philosophy and methods. These were mingled with a good deal of spite, as seen in his books as well as the interviews he condescendingly accorded to Americans from time to time.

He was the originator—or one of the originators—of the ingenious statement that Americans are "adolescent, at the twelve-year stage" (other stages also have been mentioned). It would be irreverent to assume that this statement from the pompous Austrian could have anything to do with the fact that America did not at that time lie prostrate before his throne as did Europe. But since Americans have later hastened to his banner in increasing numbers, swallowing humbly every word he uttered including this insult, it may now be timely to pry into its worth. Classification of individuals and nations in "mental age" groups is a recent digression from aptitude tests which were known throughout history and have been much amplified lately. Pure aptitude tests reached a high standard of perfection with the screening of aircraft pilots, navigators and bombardiers during World War II. They are now used in many private firms. While the principle as such is valid, the application is subtle and may often, even today, degenerate into gleeful nonsense. The "mental age" idea is a glorious example of this, bad enough when referring to individuals, worthy of nothing but the comic strip when applied to nations.

An interesting light is thrown upon this question by Dr. Oscar Brunler's recent measurements of radiations from human brains. The vibration numbers of these radiations vary from a little under 200 to above 700 "biometrics" for various persons. *But they do not change throughout the lifetime of any one person.* They have nothing to do with age. Furthermore, while a higher vibration number means a wider range of responses, it does not necessarily mean a more valuable or higher developed individual. Certain wave lengths are particularly suited to certain activities and professions. People with wave lengths from 330 to 370, for example, were found by Dr. Brunler to have particularly good intuition, while orthodoxy and right thinking is found in the higher wave lengths from 370 to 395. Above that, again, he found independent thinkers with free minds. People with "high" brain waves may lack in character and be swayed and used by people with less rapid brain waves. Again, there are constructive and destructive minds, the continuous or oscillating minds, the forceful or the weak.

Whether we accept these detailed results or not, the general picture they convey is confirmed by our daily contact with acquaintances and associates. Keen observers find no foundation for cutting across these various categories of human minds with a straight scale of "mental ages." This may be dismissed as absurd. Dr. Von Reichenback of Vienna, Dr. Kilner of St. Thomas' Hospital, London, Dr. Silvanus Thompson of Cambridge and others who demonstrated the radiations from the human body and brain, could not have been unknown to Dr. Freud. But he never embraced or worked with these more exact expressions of the mind. He confined himself to ideas and theories based partly on his experiments with patients, but to a large extent on speculations. The general picture at which he tried was therefore often erroneous, frequently ridiculous and sometimes harmful, however correctly some details were perceived.

An individual can be seen as an elastic thread stretched between facts of the past and hopes for the future. These hopes are different for each individual. Together they form the hopes of mankind. A "psychologist" can give no effective help, but may cause much harm if he has not at least a general idea of the individual's as well as humanity's entire line, from the past into the future. The wise will know his limitations and that his knowledge in these matters will be incomplete, at best. He will not be too eager to stir up the past. He may agree with the saying, "Raise not dust from the ground. It will only enter into your eyes."

Sigmund Freud and his orthodox disciples, on the other hand, insists on stirring ferociously around in the mental attics of their charges. Hardworking plodders, they don't give up until they believe they have found shocking incidents of the past, which their patients are then invited heroically to face.

In many cases retracing of the past may do good, particularly if achieved by the help of a genuine friend whose loving vibrations help lift the sufferer toward the hope of his future. Orthodox Freudists, seeing but a tiny fragment of the stretch of their patients' lives, advise against the friendly touch and loving gentleness. They think of themselves as mental surgeons, severe but able. They keep their patients' eyes fearfully, tearfully glued to real or imaginary monsters of the past. This may seem to give relief—for the first months or years. Then reaction sets in. A nauseating sense of emptiness overcomes the patient, for his life has been short-circuited.

Thirty years ago Dr. A.G. Tansely wrote in his *New Psychology* (Dodd Mead 1920) about the "stable-minded" and "unstable-minded" types of persons who got into trouble by different routes. When faced with conflicts between desire and conditions; between ideas and grim reality and all the other harassing contrasts of life, the "stable-minded" would arrange "logic-tight compartments" in their minds. They would keep the conflicting opposites segregated, no thought being permitted to escape from one to the other, just like water-tight compartments in ships. The "unstable-minded" were the more intelligent and truthful, therefore could not do this. They would use "repression." They would temporarily and conveniently forget what they could not face. Repercussions from these "repressions" would rock their insides, and the psychologists would get customers.

"But," wrote Tansley, "there is a more excellent way of dealing with conflict than either of these. If the mind is flexible and can adapt itself to experience as well as being sensitive to it, if it can endure conflict until the conflict has fought itself out, then it will eventually attain a harmony and a peace which is impossible to the other two."

Thus Tansley rose from the underworld of psychology to the realization that man is *dynamic*, his own creator. Or, he put the Sermon on the Mount into psychological wordiness, thus making it acceptable to the wordy.

Sigmund Freud only partially caught on. He saw a drive, but from the underworld only: a sexual force which occasionally boiled over and "sublimated" into mental efforts and ideals which were embarrassing abnormalities caused by a feeling of insecurity. Such a feeling enters the picture and, in time, will bring security. But Freud reversed the sequence of cause and effect. The sex force is only one—and often a minor—expression of the main life force branching out into mental, emotions, physical activities. There is little reason to worry about "repression" of one of the streams.

Through drawing heavily on religious and mystical traditions, particularly in his dream psychology, Freud had a childish fear of religion, as expressed in his diatribes against his one-time pupil, Dr. Jung.

Recently a reviewer in the *New York Times* asserted that the Freud Theory is the basis of the successful practice of the United States Army Medical Corps in the field of war neurosis. Would it not be more correct to say that a tug of war is going on between the orthodox Freudists and the broader trend of psychiatrists who feel the straight Freudian approach has done much damage and is being increasingly discredited? Many puckish G.I. patients have pitched in by gleefully pulling the leg of the Freudian practitioners during tests, thus demonstrating their own feelings in regard to these theories and methods. This does not minimize the usefulness of the general principle of delving into a person's past, which today often is done through hypnosis—a method Freud discouraged. But such retracing of the past was practiced by doctors generations before Freud and, indeed, by Plato and Pythagoras in Greece and by saints and gurus of the East and West, all down through history including chaplains in World War II! Often ancient sages and modern chaplains applied this principle more ably and subtly than the average Freudian practitioner does.

Emily Griffith, head of Denver School of Opportunity was once approached by a seventy-year-young lady who wanted to go back to kindergarten and study fairy tales. "Go back, my dear!" replied Emily confidently. "Read the Oz books. Recapture childhood. You will have the time of your life!" Mrs. Griffith, correctly, had no qualms about the reversal of "age stages" with this lady, realizing that everybody is actually all age stages all the time, the sequence of the temporary emphasis being immaterial. What would a Freudist have said? An unusually bright one might have agreed with Mrs. Griffith, but an average one would certainly not have let the old lady off that easily! What regiment of ancestors would he not have dug up as targets for this bloodthirsty oldster's murderous intent—after many expensive hours of consultation! For behind the Freudian theory looms a weird being, though never exactly defined: a "normal person" void of aspirations, dreams, or any philosophy of life, a hearty eater, drinker and performer of sex acts, holder of jobs, executor of chores, a creature developing by primly prearranged "stages"—a monster indeed, who never existed nor, we hope, ever will.

The feat of retracing the past under hypnosis is a dramatic demonstration of the science of vibration. The patient is caused to "remember" things that no longer exist in his conscious mind, or in the doctor's. The explanation is that the vibrations once created in those early years never ceased, they go on in the patient's unconscious mind forever and may be retraced. During this process the now grown patient may influence the old vibrations, straightening out twists and achieving a cure.

But often the cure will not materialize because of undue stress upon the *individual*. This is the handicap of most brands of psychology which were modern until yesterday. A newer trend peeped over the horizon in Dr. Oliver Reiser's and Mr. Blowden Davies' book *Planetary Democracy* (Creative Age Press 1940), of which the following statements are typical: "No human act is isolated. To understand any event or phenomenon, one must understand the total environment. Man must consider himself part of one single cosmic being."

Here psychology is linked with sociology, history and economics in an all-embracing science of totality. This is the viewpoint of the old-timers again. This is "retracing" *humanity's* past. Elaborating on this point, the authors wrote: "Economic security, or freedom from want, is something an enlightened civilization can attain if we put our intelligence to work on the problem."

Well, do we have an enlightened civilization? Have we put our intelligence to work on the problem? As far as production and physical amenities are concerned, yes. Elaborate researches have established that by proper development, food supply would be ample for the entire humanity, whatever the population increase. In addition to farming on land there are vast untapped resources of the oceans. Recent experiments in Scotland with "fertilizing" fiords to increase fish supplies brought most promising results. The zooplankton in the oceans is comparable to the best meat; the phytoplankton to rye flour. The United States Army has conducted experiments for taking plankton directly out of the ocean, for human food. Though there is some doubt as to the present practicability of this scheme, a future emergency would make it feasible. In addition, large oil supplies have been discovered under ocean bottoms around the United States and, also, uranium for atomic fuel as well as other distinguished minerals. The pessimists, inspired by Dr. Malthus and other misinformed authorities who talk about "overpopulation" and the necessity of reducing human numbers by wars, have no longer a worthy case. Their views are dated. If some of us do not yet enjoy freedom from want, this is not due to lack of resources. Nor is human 'greed" to blame. Nobody would have to give up present riches. By utilizing now untapped resources, all could get enough and the rich would become richer, as a general rule. Rigid and wrong ideas are the only things that would have to be given up. There are today a sufficient number of experts in every field of business and government who understand and could take proper action if authorized to do so. But the public must know how to choose experts, for these do not agree among themselves and form no coherent team. A certain education or reputation is no guarantee. The choosing and directing public must understand some essential scientific facts if they are to put the right experts in the right positions. The abundance of natural resources and their distribution must be realized. The indivisibility of science and our entire community must be sensed. Dogmas must be dropped. There is no "economic science" apart from a particular community with a definite purpose and philosophy of life. Economic "laws" are what we make them. Even Adam Smith knew this, and particularly his contemporary, Benjamin Franklin, who perhaps was an even greater economist.

Experts as well as laymen are always in danger of becoming lost along their narrow trail, or nailed to the lore of the past which, incidentally, is the only lore any education can or does teach. Therefore, only by tearing down the edifice of his training or schooling and building anew upon the ruins, again and again, may an expert become useful to the present and to the future.

Like branches of science, so individuals, too, are meaningless, lifeless, except as parts of the communities in which they function. Today this is more evident than ever before. In the stone age a single man could get along alone. Later, a family, and later again a tribe became the smallest unit that could live in comfort and provide for itself. Today almost all individual needs are supplied by our nationwide machinery of industry and farming, and, temporarily at least, our supply lines and our hearts go even beyond the national boundaries, as seen in the Marshall Plan. Philosophies claiming that man, individually is master of his own destiny have never been correct. Today, if followed, such ideas would cause disasters. Through his community, teaming with others, man may gain mastery. Alone, he would be slave, not master. The great pioneers, the tycoons of business, owe their success to nothing other than teamwork, however explosive at times.

Individual failures, on the other hand, are nearly always due to lack of teamwork, though *not* always on the part of the stricken! Periods of depression, for example, bring hardship to the innocent through a *general* lack of community teamwork, while in such periods those who still do prosper are not always the teamiest ones! The somewhat boisterous claim that psychology will save the world must, therefore, be countered with a question: *Which* psychology?

For an answer, we may again look to A.G. Tansely who in his *New Psychology* so ably psychologized the Sermon on the Mount. In another passage he wrote:

"The non-attainment of success in life owing to *external* circumstances ... has not received the attention from psychologists which its interest and importance seems to deserve."

The psychology we need today is that which will turn the individual's attention back to his community. This has not escaped the alert body of straight medical science. A picturesque example was provided by Dr. Pierre Gagey, a once-rich Paris physician who passed away in 1945. After years of observation, he concluded that eighty per cent of his patients' troubles could be traced to financial worries. Then his scientific conscience bade him test this theory by paying patients out of his private purse to overcome their difficulties. He found that these patients recovered fast, even from contagious diseases. Similar research, though not on such a Santa Clausical basis, has recently been carried out at John Hopkins Hospital, with the same result.

The need at present, therefore, is not to tickle our pride or glands, but to streamline our communities so every willing youth can look confidently to the future and marry early, with a glad heart. Thus his pride and ambition will have an outlet and his glands a chance to do what they were made for. We know that modern "business cycles" are not, like some ancient ones, caused by recurrent lack of physical resources but simply by recurrent quirks in our thinking and feeling. Although these quirks have been found to vary with the heat waves from the sun, our minds and hearts are also suns that can be made to do their bit. To bring this about may be called the immediate and most pressing task of science—of all branches of science, not merely economics, or psychology, which are nothing but vantage points from which the whole may be viewed.

The vigorous vibrations from the uninterrupted activities of ably run communities are the only real cure-alls, making the individual, as the Yogis put it: "a light, burning clearly without a flicker, like a flame on a windless night."

From there science may go on to the more subtle task of raising men to become gods. Then it may be said that science will have become religion and religion will have embraced science as it was in the olden days. So, through diversity, we will have made a long journey back to unity—a richer and more complete unity than that of old, a unity which is already in evidence in the feats of atomic fission, in the applications of the theory of relativity, in the revelation of our one world of interwoven vibrations.

CHAPTER 3

Art

To every lover of beauty, the word ART is like a caress, conjuring up rapturous colors, graceful forms, soaring music or tantalizing groupings of words. To the critic, in addition, there is a frown of disgust at all the efforts he considers inadequate, and which keep haunting his waking hours and sometimes his dreams. To the chosen few, art is the calling that prods them and tortures their souls to superhuman toil.

But to the callous scientist, art is just another expression of his swirl of vibrations, which he measures with the same incorruptible serenity as he does Winston Churchill's brain waves.

One such scientist, Dr. Oscar Brunler, has come to amazing conclusions. He claims that with his Bioscope, an instrument recently invented in France, he has measured the brain waves of the great masters of the past by means of their paintings, which still hold radiations that were once transmitted through the artists' eyes. He found that these masters had exceptional brains. Leonardo Da Vinci, he says, had the highest vibrations of any of the thousands of brains, past and present, that he has measured.

However that may be, we know that writers, musicians, painters and actors have sometimes suggested or indicated through their art, facts of nature or of human character that were rediscovered and accepted by science centuries later. Art wrested from nature its secrets. This is not always so. An artist may be mainly reproductive, portraying the beauty of nature, the known sentiments, passions and desires of man.

Such an artist may achieve the peak of fame, and there is both entertainment and education in his art. But his world may not reach beyond that of everyday thoughts and feelings. He may not extend man's vision and ambition and broaden his ideas.

There are others, whose personalities are like instruments tuned to the music of unseen worlds. They bring to man a wider horizon, a scope for development and growth. To those who appreciate them they bring a more profound enjoyment than can be derived from contemplating the record of one's own and one's neighbour's sins and follies, or even the beauties of nature. Such artists may also become great in the eyes of the world. Their gifts may be realized even while they are living on earth and their influence will then be important indeed. Often, however, their greatness is not discovered while they live. Their vision may be so wide in scope or so profound that most men do not consciously respond to their writing, their music, or their painting. In this case, are their efforts wasted? If we accept the viewpoint of vibration, we would say that not only their art but also the personalities of these artists dispatch automatically inspiring currents having a powerful although unseen effect on all human beings. Thus, even if never recognized, their art as well as the power of their personalities will reach around the world quickening the vibrations of all things and beings, continuing to do so forever. To artists who hold these views, recognition becomes a matter of minor importance.

It has been related about Tansen, a great singer of the past, that he was so shy he always preferred to sing in solitude. As he was singing one morning outside his solitary hut in the mountains, a passing traveler heard him. After having listened for a while, the traveler went up to the singer, seized his hands, deeply touched, and asked if he might bring his friend, the King, so he also might hear. The singer thanked the traveler but begged him not to bother the King or anybody else. The traveler, however, was too enthusiastic to be rebuffed so easily. He left and when he reached the palace he persuaded the King to go with him.

When the traveler returned with the King, the hut was empty and the place deserted. The singer had left for an unknown destination, never to return.

To a modern person such behaviour appears quaint and he may congratulate himself that our present singers show more appreciation of audiences. But the story divulges a sentiment familiar to every artist: his art is a sacred thing. It is like childbirth. Nobody except himself can fully understand it at the moment of creation.

The story also alludes to man's limited scope of appreciation and individual tastes. Tansen did not expect others to enjoy his singing even if one traveler did. The scope of music or art to which a person responds is usually limited to particular branches and specific expressions. Some music-lovers, for example, take it for granted that "music" means just jazz and nothing else, while others take a different viewpoint. Most people of our western civilization would think they happened into a radio hour of "noise effects" when hearing Oriental music for the first time, while after having been exposed to it continuously for a year or more, the very same people may shed tears of delight.

Others are unimpressed with any kind of music but are delighted with painting and colors which may mean nothing to many a music lover. Others again may scorn both colors and music and derive their thrills from the manner in which words are strung together in poems or prose or from the pattern of thought they convey.

Curiously, however, an interrelation appears to exist between these different expressions of art. Certain patterns of color, for example, may be seen or imagined by a person while listening to music. There are indications, not yet finally proven, of definite and impersonal relationships between such color pictures and the music inspiring them. The film *Phantasia* was suggestive of such a correlation between music and color, although it professes to give only an individual impression.

In *Electronics* September 1946, a photoelectric tone generator is described. In this instrument light beams produce pulsations in phototubes as they are flashed through holes of different patterns punched through a rotating tone wheel. These pulsations are amplified and fed to a loudspeaker and the deflecting plates of an oscilloscope. By varying the patterns of holes punched in the tone wheel, and varying the speed of rotation of the wheel, music of different qualities can be produced. The transfer from form (light) to sound is a mechanical one, yet, the instrument demonstrates the relationship between certain forms and certain kinds of sound or music. In the words of the author of the article, Mr. Lyman K. Greenness, "the instrument has answered a lot of questions concerning what and why is music."

The basic principle is the same as in old instruments: vibration, which in this instrument is produced by the rhythmic changes of light flashed through the holes of the rotating wheel and then transferred into vibrations of the deflecting plates of the oscilloscope.

Early physicists knew the relation between form and sound by a very old experiment in which thin plates of metal covered with dry sand were struck to produce certain tones. The sand then formed in definite patterns characteristic for each different tone.

When hearing and enjoying music or seeing and admiring form and color, man does not usually connect these sensations with vibration. But it is evident that in his subconscious mind these various sensations are related, though received through different organs. This may mean that in the subconscious realm of his mind, man realizes the vibratory nature of his sensations.

Also poetry and prose writings have been known to produce impressions of music or color to certain individuals, and vice versa.

Again, music, color, poetry have been successfully

employed for mental and physical healing. W. R. Hunt wrote in *Your Mind* (June 1948) about Mr. and Mrs. E. A. Boots, musicians, who had tried musical treatment on more than one thousand "mentally hopeless" individuals. Many of these could not even understand spoken words when the treatment began. Properly chosen music awakened their minds and guided them to health and usefulness, as testified by a number of doctors and psychiatrists who had sent their worst cases to the couple. Mentally brilliant, but unbalanced, people have also been successfully treated by music. Music and color schemes have been used, in part, for treatment of anemia, tuberculosis, shock. (See *Music in Medicine* by Sidney Light, MD, New England Conservatory of Music, 1946.)

According to theme and rhythm, music may be soothing, aggressive, physically, mentally or emotionally stimulating. The musicians of ancient India were keen students of these various effects of music. They evolved a certain theme or "raga" for each effect. Within these main themes they varied the melodies by inspiration of the moment. Their ancient music has been taken up again by modern Indian musicians and singers who have travelled and demonstrated to audiences all over the world that music may have physical or mental effects or may inspire love, enthusiasm, ecstasy. These tunes suggest perhaps more convincingly than casual melodies that the vibrations of music are not merely pleasant things to listen to; they are genuine food and sustenance for body and mind. Through a further development of this science of rhythm or ragas man may acquire a great new healing instrument for body and mind and an agent of education and enlightenment as well.

The fact that the ragas do not include ready-made melodies, but that the tunes are created by the artist on the inspiration of the moment, fitted to individual needs and characteristics—makes this art more alive and effective, fresh with the spirit of original creation every time it is performed.

The moment of creation is the most important time in the life of any piece or performance of art. At that time the vibrations are formed—and have their maximum strength—in the mind and in the whole personality of the artist. It is true that people may enjoy pieces of art even thousands of years after their creation and they may experience some of the joy and pain of the one-time artist at his time of creation. On the other hand, such old pieces of art may often fill the spectator with a satisfaction and a pride which turn him away from new creative efforts and may encourage a certain indifference to the present and the future, where his duties lie. The old pieces often chain the spectators and the owners to the past, to old ideas and traditions. But life is moving. Those who allow themselves too big a dose of the luxury of reminiscence will drop from the caravan and be left behind. What is worse, they will delay others as well.

The worship of old pieces of art may give rise to monstrous misjudgements, as for instance when people look complacently at the bombing of cities whereby thousands of people are killed or maimed—but raise their voices in fiery protest when old monuments are hit! To cause suffering to one single human child is worse than destroying all monuments of art. Destruction of art treasures may serve the good purpose of tearing man's mind loose from the dead past, and from his pride, and turn his attention and efforts to creation, which is the highest purpose of art.

Historians may lament such a point of view, since the old pieces of art are important sources of knowledge about the past. Their case is a worthy one, though these energetic people have proven able to unearth and restore the most heavily damaged pieces. Besides, they have other sources of knowledge—even discounting the prediction that, in the not too distant future we may be able to establish a direct vibratory link with the vibrations of the past, which live on forever. Some modern historians seem to have been in touch, consciously or not, with these swirls of the past. The Austrian, Dr. Egon Friedell, for example, describes a distant past of which we have no record with such convincing clarify and so many amazing details that more than mere guessing is apparent.

At different periods of history artists have been called upon to work for different purposes and reasons. Sometimes they were rarely called upon at all. They were left to starve or abandon their art. In other periods, practically every man and woman was an artist at painting, weaving, music or poetry. Far from taking the bread away from professional artists, this made them flourish. With every man and woman an artist, good art was appreciated. Ample allowances were offered to gifted artists so they could devote all their time to their creative work.

Among these periods were the heyday of ancient Greece, the time of King Asoka in India, the Renaissance period in Europe. Some of these periods were also materially well-balanced, with an even and ample supply of good food, rich clothing and beautiful homes, churches and public buildings. Farmers and craftsmen in the German and Italian Renaissance towns and cities were regularly seen with silver buttons on their jackets and gold and silver buckles on their shoes. The craftsmen's guild voted big sums of money for art in churches, schools and other public buildings.

To say that the bloom of art was simply the result of the material well-being would be as superficial as presuming that art alone was responsible for the perpetual boom during these long periods. There was no doubt an interaction. Wealth and leisure made it easy and natural to support art. On the other hand, art influenced the pattern of the community. Good art teaches a sense of proportion and values which help solve even social and financial problems. During the Renaissance period, whatever riches a man collected were real things—land, houses, clothes, art. There was not much opportunity to hoard money. The different cities had different money tokens, most of them underweight and often arbitrarily withdrawn and changed by the rulers. This may have been accidental, but it seemed in keeping with the spirit of the time, valuing the real things while money, the *token* of wealth, came second. The result—unexpected by some—was a general living standard higher than at any other time.

It may be impossible to say which was the original impulse—art, religion, a material boom or a financial or monetary system or lack of system, but all these factors seemed to work together in achieving an art that became a lasting inspiration.

During the first decades of the industrial age, art was practically banned from the life of the majority and chased into a few well-to-do homes where it was still appreciated in a tame way. Most artists were pariahs, beggars, unwanted ones who did not make money and were thrown out of girls' homes by angry fathers. The artists starved and so did their art. The demand for the glorification of a few fortunate homes was not inspiring. A few exceptions to this rule in England and Scandinavia did not alter the main trend.

Eventually art conquered new fields of its own related to the industrial age: radio, motion pictures, television, of which some productions will wield a power and influence upon contemporary society as mighty as the great Renaissance art, and influence the future even more.

With the growth of the industrial community, its masters knocked on the doors of art with demands for decoration of their new symbols of power: factories, business buildings, banks. At long last art was asked to take a hand in the more important things: the houses ordinary people lived in, the streets and cities they walked and worked in. The meaning of art was raised from mere decoration to basic creation and designing of fundamental plans, the arrangement of rooms and gadgets in a home, the distribution of houses, streets, parks and playgrounds in a city.

The artists of the future may be increasingly occupied with such basic tasks. The home of the poorest citizens may be planned and built by great artists, for the homes are the community's face towards its members. The home carries a message to every baby born there and is the first educational impulse from the community to the newcomer. As this new citizen grows up, his proper education requires continuous contact with art. In modern education children express their individual natures and tell their stories through paintings and drawings. On this basis can be determined the music, color and activity suited to each individual.

The whole problem of education may be called a matter of art—in medical and educational science. Good educators, good doctors and psychologists—have to be artists in spirit, in order to feel or sense the changing needs of their pupils or patients. And do not artists have to be both psychologists and educators in order to fulfill their creative and distributive missions?

Again, artists may be called upon to assist in the world of politics, finance and international relationships, for in the artist's mind is that rhythm and sense of proportion, which form the basis of creation and is the essence of all its expressions.

As rhythm, grace and harmony are realized by dancers in the physical world, so art has been called the manifestation of a dancing soul.

Chapter 4

Education

William Shakespeare saw this world as a stage, on which all men are actors. But is there a purpose behind the wobbling drama? If so, could it be—education? Henry Ford appeared to have such an idea in mind when he said, "My only fortune is my experience." Compared to this treasure, a billion dollars did not seem worth mentioning.

If the whole purpose of life is education—of man and beast and plant and the whole universe, then we are faced with a humbling fact: we do not know the first thing about it. We have no clear idea about such a comprehensive purpose of life, hence we cannot know what sort of education we ought to have to lead us toward it. There are individuals who believe they know, but humanity as a whole, its institutions, science, art, literature, does not know of such a purpose.

This at once scales down the scope of education but extends its span of time. Obviously, we cannot even hope to reach any "perfect" or "complete" system of training in homes, schools and colleges and, since even adults know but little about the final goal, we are all in it, we are all pupils, from birth to the grave.

Even if this realization may hurt our pride, it is a refreshing one and greatly helpful in making the best rather than the worst of the situation. It rids us, from the start, of the boasters who tell us they know everything about our tots and how they should be "handled."

It makes us keenly sympathetic to three wise kings of yore who came to the cradle of a baby to worship. After centuries of conceit, wise men are again today worshipping at the cradles of babies, while grown-ups are the pupils. This does not mean that the babies, as a group, have any final answer to our problems. But they have a very definite message to convey which, formerly, we ignored, in spite of suggestions and advice thousands of years ago.

A dazzling dome of glass is the proud possession of the Clinic of Child Development at the Yale University School of Medicine. It is so constructed that one can see from outside in but not from inside out. Around this dome stand daily and sometimes nightly white-haired scientists, peppy young nurses and doctors, with notebooks ready, watching worshipfully His Majesty the Child who is occupied within his dome with toys or clay or painting or just nothing. The child is conducting the serious business of growing up, unaided and undirected by adults. From the expressions on his face, from his movements, his work with toys or clay or color, conscientious observers have gathered hints of a purpose and a plan toward which the little child is working and which mysteriously have been instilled in his mind without any adult aid. These scientists and nurses, whose job it is to learn at the feet of babies and children, will tell you that they have found a sort of fountain of life. They keep young and happy and unspoiled by constantly watching the wonder of the child. They begin to realize the hazy outline of a purpose and a plan themselves. Increasingly they have come to discard the old theory that children are products of environment and heritage only. Both these influences exist, but they have been overestimated in comparison with a third factor that was not even recognized by science until recently: there seems to be a source of inspiration and orderly wisdom from which each baby or child draws according to its individual requirements and talents. The old folks called it "soul" or "spirit." It can be seen in the concentrated eagerness with which the child goes about its important business of developing. Sometimes this eager, frank and non-compromising concentration stays with an individual beyond childhood. He may retain his keen sight and sense while being knocked about in offices and classrooms, on subway trains, at crowded lunch bars where he gulps a cup of coffee and two hot dogs—the only lunch he can afford. He may go through life as absorbed in it and as unspoiled as he was in childhood, and may thus become a great man or woman. More often, however, the exhausting strife for mere survival, or of booze, or for keeping up with the Joneses sidetracks him at an early age, dulling his wits, chilling his heart, blurring the light in his eyes. He forgets that he was once hurrying to fulfill a purpose of life. He denies there ever was such a purpose. Then he goes about "educating" his child!

But wait. Victims of rock-throwing urchins in our city streets may well ask indignantly if these are to be our idols. No, rock-throwing is not commendable, but even this conveys to us a message in the form of a question: what did we do to this child that turned him into a rock-thrower? He did not start throwing rocks in the cradle! It is a good bet he never was under the dome at Yale or in the care of another worshipful expert. Could somebody have produced in him a feeling that he was a helpless prisoner in a cage where some big apes were constantly prodding him to do silly tricks, by scolding, slapping or spanking him, or asking him that fateful, nonsensical question, "Why did you do it?" Suppose you were this child, feeling so helpless in your cage, not knowing one ape from another, and then you found some rocks on the floor...?

The story of nine-year-old Henry Johnson was told in *Science Illustrated*, January 1948. Henry did not throw rocks when he first was taken to a child expert at Columbia University Teacher's College in April, 1947. He stammered, and the expert thought he was rather too well-behaved. Stammering is often caused by repression and confusion. After weekly interviews or rather play-hours in the expert's office, Henry became gradually less well-behaved. In October he clouted the expert over the head with a rolled-up finger painting. Incidentally he had quit stammering. The expert was very pleased with this clout over the head, although it did not mark the termination of the treatment. But it signified that the boy's repressed emotions were coming out into the open. He was back on the trail of his natural self. He was again in touch with the mysterious source of life from which parental busybodies had shut him off.

Babies are not angels or devils, neither are they copies of parents and surroundings, but each one appears to have a particular and unique message to deliver, or try to deliver. In the past they rarely succeeded. In pre-war Germany, for example, an obstinate conspiracy of grown-ups, rather than listen to, bullied their youngsters into Nazi strait-jackets and made them unleash World War II. In America, England and the Scandinavian countries, a conceited brotherhood of overgrown-ups ignored with equal haughtiness the aspirations of the young, pushing them gently into fragile glass houses of peace movements and frightened neutrality. The awakening was painful. When the youngsters found the make-believe world of their elders shattered around them, they also found that they had to throw not mere rocks, but steel and flames and plutonium—to survive. If the young had been permitted to grow unhampered, as they now do in the Yale dome, Nazism and similar ulcers might never have developed. Youngsters would have become more correctly tuned to the world in which they lived. Robbers and murderers could have been detected and stopped before they had time to gang up on the rest of the world.

How are we to listen to the youngsters' messages? Not every home can have a glass dome. But there are other means of communication. First, there are the notes of those who watched the dome, available in book form. There are many other good books. A recent one is *Painting and Personality: A study of young children,* (Chicago University Press, 1947.) In this book two women scientists, Mrs. Rose H. Alschuler and Dr. Laberta W. Hattwick, reported their findings after having studied children' paintings and drawings for ten years. From various forms and colors dotted on paper by four-year-olds and up, the authors were able to read mental and physical conditions, conflicting emotions and thoughts. Yellow, for example, was usually found to express happiness, as, incidentally, it does in folklore as well as in what has been considered superstition in many countries. Blue indicated worry and anxiety in a very small child; self-control in an older child. Various shades of red denoted strong emotions, love or hate. Often one color was covered by layers of other colors, which would denote repression of the emotions expressed by the first color. These studies will help parents understand their children and also may provide clues for devising color schemes suitable to various types for influencing and correcting their emotional life. So far such efforts have been guesswork to a large extent. These studies of drawings also throw light on childrens' stages of development. Books on education divide the years of a child into definite stages with different emphasis about which there has been no agreement. Some hold that all basic traits are formed between the ages of two and five, while others put more stress on later stages. One well known statesman, having achieved his success in life by good guesses, was thoroughly convinced that the age period between six and nine was the most important. During this time he insisted on being with his boy as much as possible. He said the age period from two to five was "mind-forming" while the time elapsing between six and nine was character-forming! The entire problem of stages may become clearer and more certain by the observation of drawings.

Apart from books and works of experts, are there ways of getting at a child's mind directly? Some parents are helped by a keen memory by which they can recall their own childhood. Those who cannot may gradually get results by watching the expression in the child's face and eyes. In trying to assume that same expression, an observing parent may begin to feel the thoughts and emotions that prompted it. In similar manner parents may watch the child's posture, movements, grimaces and then try to copy these and figure out what emotions and thoughts may have caused such movements. The hard-trying adult will look perfectly ridiculous doing so, and he will feel most refreshed by being, for once, outside and beyond himself in an effort to get inside another human mind. When he thinks he has the right answer, he may check with a book or two. He may have to endure some disappointments, but after a while he will be amazed at the accuracy of his assumptions, if he has any flair for this game at all. Many arrive at a stage where they trust their own judgment more than any book's. They then share the experience of some educators and child doctors who feel they have become able to enter the mind of the child and view things from his standpoint. They have acquired two states of consciousness between which they can alternate at will; their own, and that of the person they are observing. This, also, was the secret of the ancient "wise men"—the teachers, gurus, in the East and in the West.

Granted that we have now become able to listen in to the child's messages whether as teachers, doctors or just parents, then what? We have been instructed and educated by our youngster. Can the process now be reversed? Even if we do not know the final aim and purpose of his life, or our own, isn't there something we can teach him?

Whatever the child's ultimate aim and purpose may be, he has to live and function in the world we have made for him. He may change that world in his own good time, but only if he can master it first. We proceed proudly to teach him this mastery. There are pitfalls along this road. We may go too far or fall short. We may be too bold or too timid. But there is one reassuring fact: the child is adaptable. He can take a lot of wrong education and still do pretty well. He has taken a whale of misinformation and spoiling and maltreatment and beating from parents and teachers all through history. Yet, he is still going strong. The average American youngster of today is probably the best ever to have grown up on this globe. He is as a rule happier, more cooperative, efficient and thoughtful than perhaps any of his forebears. Incidentally, he is also the most successful soldier in battle, the most able defender of his rights. Can these facts be traced to a trend in American education?

Knowing that everybody wallows in mistakes, most Americans try to do all their educational sinning one way: to be too lenient rather than too strict, to give the child too much rather than too little freedom, to draw forth his hidden qualities even if some of them may be "bad"—rather than suppress the "bad" with the good. This is not a new idea. It has been launched, on and off, in many European countries; in England, Soviet Russia, India, South America. But it has never been applied so extensively and consistently as in the United States. In prewar Germany, on the other hand, youngsters were subjected to the most rigid discipline, including whipping and beating. The result: Nazi Germany with its sadism and concentration camps!

Should this be a warning against even milder forms of slapping and spanking? Obviously there is a difference only in degree. There are still, even today, American psychologists calling themselves child experts who brazenly tell us "Educational Science" approves of "a little spanking," as if there is or ever will be a body of infallible scientist-supermen in this subtle field! It is safe to hazard the guess that these "experts" have no keen memory so have never been able to remember their own reaction when and if their parents first "spanked" them. American parents may slap a child in moments of impatience and the culprits may be none the worse for it, but luckily they do not accept this procedure as a principle. King Solomon's contention that the spanking of one's child was a sign of one's love was typical of the old tyrants and cannot have made a hit with the average American who does not think too highly of kings whiling away their time with slave girls anyway.

While normal, healthy children won't degenerate because of an occasional slapping, a "problem child" may get seriously disturbed. This is why education must be taken so seriously. A healthy child can stand almost any kind of education, or lack of one. But to save the border cases from harm, wise parents would want to be careful; would want to try to avoid slapping and spanking altogether. Sometimes one hears the brash statement, "A little spanking will just tune the youngster to the knocks and blows of real life!"

No, wise guy, real life does not give that kind of knocks and blows. Real life does not whip a man on his "behind"—except in lands with concentration camps in the charge of sadists. Real life, in America, has a standard of dignity which is being violated when a child is spanked—by grown-up brutes, who thus established themselves as the law, with no appeal.

Real life has other kinds of knocks and blows which parents have a right and sometimes a duty to apply. If an adult proves inadequate in his community, he will meet the chilled wall of indifference. If the case is bad he will be without a job. If still more serious, he may be removed, temporarily, from society. Parents' first reaction to an erring child would be to turn away in sorrow, making it clear that the youngster has hurt them. If this is not enough, then "the chill" may be put on. It would be a tough and rare youngster who would not come rushing back very soon. He will feel that he has broken the tie of affection that was the mainstay of his life by his own actions. This will set him pondering. He may try his parents' endurance. He may even run away. Let him! Comparing the great chill of the outside world with his home will do him good. When he comes back, ask no questions! His return is sufficient answer to all questions. Everything will be as before.

At the same time, thoughtful parents will look for the causes behind their children's "bad" behaviour. There may be physical or mental ailments. This is one more reason why slapping is so inadvisable, and may even be inadvertently cruel. A gentle and cautious attitude, making all the mistakes on the spoiling side, may make a fair success even of a child who does have undiscovered or incurable ailments.

A story comes to my mind about a girl, Martha, who was not to be blessed with this right sort of education until she was forty years old. Even then it worked wonders. No teachers or parents, but just a small American community in which she arrived from abroad, provided for her the conditions and the atmosphere that changed her life.

Martha grew up in one of the small countries of Europe where people work hard and expect much of each other. Her parents were unusually able, energetic and talented, well established in their community. They were also kind, honest, well-intentioned. The mother, being a former school-teacher, undertook to teach Martha herself as she had done successfully with her other children. To her amazement and dismay, Martha seemed to have no talents, no ability, no initiative, no interest—"no nuthin." Both parents cajoled her, scolded her and, when she was of age, pushed her into jobs—from which she promptly returned. They were unable even to make her do small chores in the home. They sought advice of educators and psychologists who could only caution them to take it easy. Everybody understood it was a case of natural reaction and hopelessness of a child against too able and eager parents. In addition, she probably had ailments which, however, were not discovered. This diagnosis helped nobody. Apart from the short intervals when she was trying daily to hold down a job, she stayed home, unable to do anything useful, a nightmare to her parents, a nightmare to herself.

Then her parents died and a relative invited her to America. He thought that the completely different surroundings might possibly change her and draw forth whatever latent qualities she might possess. She did not come to New York or Chicago, where sooner or later she might have met people from home, but far away—to a farm on the West Coast. She came into surroundings where not a trace was left of her unlucky past and where no energetic parent prodded her to efforts beyond her power. Even her relative kept in the background, feeling humbly that he might form a slight link with her past. He never alluded to her former home in any way.

One of the most heartening and touching American traits is that glad expectation and genuine courtesy with which a newcomer is met. Curiously, in Europe there is a widespread belief that the well-known American efficiency makes the American people heartless robots, exploiting immigrants to their last drop of sweat and simply crushing the inefficient ones. The very opposite is true. American efficiency is not merely mechanical; it extends to the human field as well. Consequently, newcomers are accepted with whatever talents and standards of efficiency they may possess. They are left to develop their powers in their own good time, assisted by the community's encouragement, appreciation, understanding. Americans in the small and genuine communities do not look down upon, or up to, but straight at—each other. They looked straight at Martha too, made her feel just like one of them, in her full and equal rights as a human being and worker. They expected of her nothing but what she could give. They made her forget she had been "different," "inefficient," "impossible." They even made her feel a little better than average, because they were impressed with her humility and the gratefulness she showed toward her new country. The only type of newcomers who may encounter difficulty in America are the ones who are too boastful about their own past and their old country. Martha had nothing to boast of, nothing she even cared to remember. Like the old pioneers, she had fled her own country to come to the better land and this land embraced her. The hard and painful knots in her mind loosened in the atmosphere of respect and friendship. Through a little bit of "spoiling" Martha became a happy and increasingly useful citizen of the new world. She now drives a dashing car of recent vintage bought from money entirely earned by herself.

And then there is the story of Fred, who perhaps was spoiled a bit too much. At the age of seventeen he was known as a "wolf" of poor discrimination and unattractive methods. He was rapidly heading for the sort of reputation that might impede his entire career. One night his father invited a friend, a psychiatrist, to have dinner with himself and the boy. This doctor was a really genuine psychologist and, incidentally, a good story teller. After having won the ear of Frank with some good yarns, he invited the boy with his father to visit him at the hospital the next day.

When they arrived, the doctor introduced them to some of his patients. These seemed to be in fairly good health physically, but the restless eyes and the way they talked and walked betrayed their confused minds and jittery nerves. They had become tragedies to their families and themselves and useless to their community. Their existence was worse than death. No explanation was given until Frank asked about the causes for these conditions. Then the doctor went through a few cases. Some appeared to have been driven too hard. Others had been given too much leeway. Now, such mistakes did not always lead to disaster, said the doctor, but these had lost hold of their steering devices and were just following their impulses blindly, with no effort at self-control.

"We believe we can mostly cure the body in our day," said the doctor, "but with all our psychology we cannot cure the minds or the emotions, except when the patient pitches in to help us. Man is still responsible in the world of mind, and these patients"—the doctor made a sweeping gesture—"are only a few extremes among millions of unhappy cases in homes and at working places."

Fred paled. Then his eyes narrowed and he looked suspiciously at the doctor. "You are just kidding! I know—you want to scare me into being a 'good boy'!"

The doctor looked squarely at him. "I will take you up on that, Fred! If you are not just a big mouth, you would not want to throw such accusations at me without proof. I was giving you a chance to get the facts. You will study medicine—psychiatry—go as far as I have, and further, if you can. Then you may come back and talk!"

Now, what other ending could this story have than that Fred became an outstanding psychiatrist who now loves to warn his students and his patients by telling them about the follies of his own youth? Particularly does he like to praise his former teacher who saved him from misery in the nick of time! Also, he thinks children should learn early about love, family life, and all connected matters. He blames his own early exuberance, partly, on lack of such instruction and on the bits of half-knowledge he received from other boys while they were planning "great adventures."

In my home my mother began telling me very truthfully about childbirth and everything related to it when I was five. She just answered as correctly as she could all my questions. When, at the age of twelve, my boy friends began whispering in the corners, I shrugged and told them the whole story as I had heard it from my mother. They gasped. Once a male teacher came along and heard what we were talking about. He reported to my home that I was "entertaining the other boys with lurid information." My father came with me to school next morning and gave the teacher a piece of his mind in front of myself and all the other boys. The teacher fidgeted, tried to interrupt, "B-but please, let's get the children out of here while we are speaking about these things!"

"Not at all!" shot back my father. "I want them to hear every word of it! I believe that will do them good."

None of us seemed to suffer any harm by this frankness. These boys of my class are all good citizens now, most of them married, none of them divorced.

But the procedure raises another intriguing question: what about my father barging in and arguing with the teacher in front of all the boys? Shouldn't the various educators in home and school form a united front of agreement toward the child? This is what many experts tell us even today. My father dared to disagree. "A united front," he said, "is something we adopt toward a common enemy. Is the child a common enemy?"

I may not have been entirely without guilt in respect to this heresy on the part of my parents. Once, eight years old, I heard my mother whisper to my father about this principle of "agreement in front of the child," just as he was coming to my aid in a dispute. They did not know I had overheard the remark, so they flushed when I offered this contribution, "Well, you may agree—or you may be honest. Which will it be?"

They looked at each other, smiled, then proceeded to be honest.

If this attitude be generally accepted, it will solve many hitherto unsolved problems. There has been much talk about teaching young children more sociology, economics and a general understanding of the workings of the community. Scattered efforts in that direction have been made but, since even the grown-ups do not agree on the fundamentals of such sciences, what could we teach our young?

If our line would be to skip the cagey "agreement" plan and stick to honesty, the answer would be simple. We would have to present the various viewpoints. We could not brush children off with "digests." Would not this create confusion? This opposition has proven wrong. Confusion is rather promoted by the schoolbooks pompously proclaiming one thing, and then the children hearing other things at home or at a meeting. They cannot have all possible viewpoints at school, but a fair selection and a broadminded outlook. The various viewpoints and discussions around them will greatly increase interest. Children love arguments. And if there is too much to digest, the child's mind will simply take in what it can assimilate and skip the rest for the time being.

But such procedure raises another question: Which teacher would be able to present these different viewpoints within the various sciences? Not one! The children could not depend upon regular teachers for such information. The leading experts in various fields would have to present their views via broadcasts or books. In the field of mechanics, a similar procedure has already been adopted in many American schools. Automobile mechanics, watchmakers, aircraft hands mix with the children at the work benches in school during the hours of "adult education." Thus the youngsters meet the real experts and workers. Would it be too much to demand such community service, occasionally, from all professions? The advantage would be mutual. The business manager or banker by trying to explain his problems to the children would thereby understand them better himself. I can think of many senators and congressmen who would be loved by children and make them really understand the problems of statesmanship. I can think of others who would be heartlessly razzed by insolent youngsters and would go back to their politics no worse for the treatment.

There is the other course of giving the children only one officially authorized line. This is the Nazi and Communist method of education. The youngsters are fed the "right" opinions from which there must be no digression. Honesty has been sacrificed in favour of "agreement." The child is never asked, just as Mr. Common Citizen is never asked.

The line of honesty does not merely have the advantage of maintaining confidence between the grown-ups and the child. It also develops his discrimination and judgment. Occasionally children may even see more clearly than grown-ups. Putting our problems and disagreements before them means augmenting our counsel with keen young minds, which may help us as much as we help them. The question "When should we start putting problems before the child?" may be answered with the classic line: it is never too early—never too late!

But should not the youngster be spared such heavy ammunition? Isn't he entitle to live "the carefree life of a child?" Rose H. Alschuler and Laberta W. Hattwick wrote in the above-mentioned book, *A Study of Young Children* (Chicago University Press 1947): "Acute problems characterize the lives of young children just as they do the lives of adults." Those who can remember their own childhood would tend to replace the words "just as" with "much more than." My own childhood problems seem to be mountain-heavy compared to the usually lightweight worries of adult life. Even wartime combat service did not affect me as seriously and violently as some childhood dilemmas.

What were the crushing burdens of these childhood problems? The fervent wish to grow up, to find my place in the world and to help—were frustrated by lack of information and sometimes apparent lack of cooperation. Nothing would have been more helpful in this quest than greater frankness and confidence on the part of grown-ups.

Putting it in vibratory terms, the children are seeking to adjust and coordinate their vibrations with the pattern intended for them in the universal scheme, while grown-ups too often treat them as just roving rascals, content to play and throw rocks through windows. But even the rock-throwing, to the child, may be a seriously plotted scheme to overthrow a tyrannical Nazi dynasty of grown-ups at the risk and peril of being tortured!

Jumping now to the youth in actual Nazi countries, such as prewar Germany, what made the youngsters fall for the Nazi doctrines? Above all the appeal to service, the idea that now, at last, youth was called upon to play a part in the real world of the grown-ups. For generations they had been considered just nuisances, while they had harboured lofty dreams of heroic sacrifice! So, while the Nazi theories were duly doubted and scorned by the German youth, as any uniformly imposed theory would have been, the challenging call to service and sacrifice won the battle and swept them along. But, as they invaded and ravaged small and formerly happy and prosperous countries, doubts were back again with full fury, as evidenced in their conversations with the "conquered" and in numerous mutinies or efforts at revolt. This was the beginning of the real "re-education" of the Germans, which can be successfully carried through only by the humble who realize that every one of us is in need of "re-education." On such basis the Germans and we others might get together on quite a scheme of mutual enlightenment.

The statements that youth is raring to serve and to sacrifice itself for the community may be challenged by parents who have just tried in vain to persuade their young hopeful to mow the lawn. Now, if this hopeful one had been in Naziland, he would have been successfully persuaded by rod or waving flags to mow that lawn, if such was the will of the Feuhrer. We are considering the opposite kind of community which, purposefully, gives him a certain freedom of choice. Any parent who would try to go through the physical and mental exertions of the younger set throughout an average day, would end up with aching limbs and exhausted brain. They would not charge laziness! But, faced with lawn-mowing and 1001 other pressing propositions, the youngsters may feel that the former must wait in the interest of the most urgent softball game or any important outing that will acquaint him with trees and lakes. This does not mean that lawns should not occasionally be mowed. It is even being possible for clever parents to make such a task appear attractive and acceptable, although sometimes by means bordering on bribery and blackmail. If confidence is established by uncompromising honesty and loving, but not clinging, care on the part of parents, and if this confidence be not drawn upon too heavily, youngsters are apt to grab at an opportunity for doing useful chores. They should be so chosen that they occasionally challenge to the utmost the mental and physical agility of the youngster. Otherwise they will appear dull and unattractive. Also, the child has a right to get bored and tired. Steadfastness belongs to a later age.

Granted that the basis of our educational system is a humble supposition that there is an ultimate purpose of life which as a community we do not know; that therefore the youngster must be given freedom to find his own bearings and develop according to his individual requirements; that school and universities should concentrate on teaching him how to function in this world and master it so he can make a living and have a background—have we succeeded in these aims? Have we found the right balance? Have we provided the best possible setting for the individual's triumphant march toward his unknown goal?

Once, at the age of 19, while I was studying hard to become a civil engineer, I read an advertisement in a paper about a wonderful "professor" in a far and distant land who would be willing to part with secret instructions on how to control mind and emotions, stay eternally healthy, obtain hypnotic power and master telepathy—all this for a mere trickle of five dollars! Before my engineering studies, I had sniffed at philosophy, medicine and psychology. I had a general knowledge of many branches of science. But none of them had offered to control my mind or emotions or help me heal myself. The advertisement appeared insincere and in bad taste, but still it bored into my mind, insistently and painfully like a harpoon. I talked it over with parents and friends, among others a cousin who was a prominent man of letters, an educator and an editor. He chided me thunderously for paying attention to such nonsense. Yes, I ended up by sending for the "instructions!" They were as crude as the advertisement. But they represented my first fumbling step along an intriguing road leading to many organizations of varying degrees of respectability and sincerity. Gradually was revealed to me a world of which school or college had said nothing. The fact that such advertisements could appear and seriously interest numbers of well educated youngsters seemed to indicate a lack in our educational system, a vacuum that could be exploited by charlatans. Later my paths crossed more mature and sincere organizations and individuals offering similar advice and counsel. Even though none could give complete satisfaction, they established the existence of a world that had been neglected. It could be described as awareness—of body, mind, emotions. The training offered most of us so far does not go down to this fundamental awareness and therefore is not effective. Boxers or football players are supposed to undergo most profound physical training. But even they know but little about breath control, nerve building, tactically nothing about direction of digestion. The mind is more seriously neglected. Filling it with stuff is not training. Reading books, listening to lectures may drag it along in this sort of activity, it may also make it more dull. To probe into the elements of mind and build it up is a different matter. Even more important is the control and direction of emotions.

Today America is beginning to feel this vacuum. Researchers at Chicago, Columbia, Princeton, Yale Universities have descended from science's previous throne of indifference to investigate beyond the orthodox realms. Dr. Joseph B. Rhine of Duke University has even experimented with communication between minds, clairvoyance, telepathy. (*The Reach of Your Mind*, William Sloane, 1948, review in *Your Mind*, June 1948). By assisting such material in building from the ground up, a dynamic science of mind and emotions may become established. When this has been expressed in education, a civilization may arise which may make this present one look like gay barbarism. The keynote may be the science of vibration which, if adopted as a hypothesis, would be a useful guiding light even from the start.

Among the results achieved so far is the realization of willpower, not as a ferocious dragon, but a gentle suave diplomat. Material and social success, scholastic results and self-healing against heavy odds have been achieved, not by storming ahead but by subtle and consistent wishing. It has long been in good taste to chide optimists for what is called "wishful thinking". If this line be turned around to "thoughtful wishing" it represents quite a power.

The thoughtful wishes of an individual sets vibrations in motion which continue to work on the individual as well as on his community like insistent press agents in the field. However, even the most able agents will not succeed if their goods are not eventually wanted by the community. We come back to the old truth: the individual is merely an interwoven part of the whole. He can achieve miracles if he wishes in accordance with the larger wish. He will achieve nothing if his line of wishes are too far removed from that of the community, whether better or worse. This community, again, is merely part of humanity and the universe. Thus, the first requisite for real success is that one can say honestly, as in the prayer, "Thy will be done."

Even though we do not know the final aim and purpose of life, the science of vibration may already have convinced us of the indivisibility of the whole. For the educator it would seem both safe and proper, therefore, to convey this idea to the child. This is also a part of making him master of this world. The all-embracing, ever present BEING in whom and by the breath of whom we live, is the answer to the other questions. There are additional details to be achieved or mastered, but this keynote would seem the most important. In the light of this vision, the proper cultivation of emotions, mind and body may be understood and carried out.

In the light of this vision only, the sciences of sociology, history, law, economics, medicine, psychology, physics, geology, chemistry, derive meaning and significance. They are merely gateways to the knowledge of The ONE. The more serious mistakes committed by the sciences, as well as striking mistakes and failures in education, appear to spring from lack of such realization.

At which age should a child first be introduced to this ONE BEING, his father and mother and source of life? Again this old line may be the proper answer: it is never too early–never too late. The entire process of education consists in the influence of this ONE BEING's vibrations upon the vibratory system that is the baby child (or the adult child.) When one's mind and heart have been focused upon the source of all inspiration, then, like the needle of a compass, so will all other activities and studies point in that one direction.

Can there be any greater single task for the educator than bringing about this direction of attention—in the child and in himself? But this requires self-control and even self-sacrifice. Any proudly prepared overall educational scheme may have to be changed or abandoned altogether. For the children are pioneers, similar in many ways, yet each one carrying a special message to the world in which he is born. Although nobody, perhaps, can tell at first what this message is, or what should be carefully tended and what should be rooted out in a child's disposition and character, the watchful educator will listen to every word that comes his way, giving it a chance to develop and deliver its message, for he knows he is dealing with the Life of God.

Chapter 5

Everyday Life

For situations and challenges of everyday life are the real teachers of wisdom. They are also the tests. The fortitude, kindness and resourcefulness with which man meets the situations of everyday life are the only proofs of maturity or personality. Sermons and scriptures of religion are only comments or explanations of the real teachings hidden in the circumstances of life. A man's creed or belief is a passing fancy of little importance. He may retain his belief while growing in wisdom, or may want to change it, which need cause no weeping. Some people fear losing a belief or creed, but whatever man "loses" in this world, there is always something better to gain. Evolution favors change.

True, all religions emphasize the virtue of faith, but faith is something over and beyond belief or creed. A man who has faith in himself, and his fellow man, and his cause, his country—in God—can accomplish things; nay, his faith is the very power that drives him on and drives others to him; it is the spirit that unites and creates. Faith it was which made man venture out on the ocean in little boats for the first time. Faith is what enables a boy to dive from a high platform or set out for a ski jump. Faith was what made a Caesar conquer the world. Faith was what made an almost unarmed island people stem the tide of another would-be world conqueror and his warriors. Of one who has complete faith it has been said symbolically that he walks upon the waters of life. He who has a little faith may manage to swim, while he who has no faith will drown. Because he who has faith attains calmness of mind and a contagious, carefree happiness, it has been said symbolically that he stills the storm—that is, the storm of doubt and worry in the heart of himself and others.

The word "doubt" does not here apply to religious traditions or dogmas. Such doubt is healthy and stimulating. The doubt to be overcome is the doubt that one can accomplish the thing one has set out to do—doubt in oneself and one's fellow. That doubt is overcome by knowledge, by determination and work—all of which spring from love.

In factories, shipyards, shops and offices and on farms men and women are making cars, washing machines, ships, engines, foodstuffs, questionnaires and regulations. Ships are useful to carry food to hungry people, but apart from that they have a message to convey to men. They are products and proofs of faith. They are also products of knowledge, but even this knowledge was acquired in a spirit of faith that prompted research and perseverance. Again, love of achievement and common action caused men to cooperate in the production. The ship is proof of men's ability to get along among themselves and do things together which no single man could do alone. Nor could all the men in the world achieve this if they did not cooperate and divide the work between them, if they did not sacrifice the vain idea of making a ship single-handed. Of the finished product the marine engineer can be rightly proud—and so can the boy who swept the floor in one of the factories. However much it they may have argued in the process, the fact that the ship is launched is a proof of sacrifice, cooperation and faith.

Then the brave sailors take it over. None of them could run the ship single-handed. Nor could a hundred men run it if everyone insisted upon being master. They come together and form an organization—a team. However much they may resent things and disagree, the fact that the ship reaches its destination in a minimum of time is an outstanding achievement and evidence of a certain moral and emotional maturity of humanity.

These fields of human activity are genuine places of

worship. They are also most efficient universities in which men are trained in the art of living. Here they learn the essentials of philosophy, economics, morality, faith and love. The stokers, deckhands, officers, engineers and masters are all of them teachers, professors and pupils at the same time in these universities.

So much for the group as a whole. What about individual differences? As we know, there is a gradation according to responsibility ranging from unskilled hands to managers and presidents, from cabin boys to masters, from raw recruits to top-kicks and on up. But there is another quite different and distinct gradation according to the team spirit of everyone, or his "faith". Some are "cooking with gas" whatever position they occupy. If within the ranks of labor, such a one may be picked as representative to the union because of the confidence he inspires. Then again, Mr. so-and-so may prefer his stooges for such jobs and get them elected by tricks known to the trade, thus by-passing men of quality. As a general rule, ranks, positions, income gradations, including ranks and gradations in labor unions or employers' organizations, constitute a kind of mock hierarchy, a beautiful game, not representing any true gradation of quality. *But* these mock hierarchies are *indicative* of a real thing: a gradation of real personal qualities, which never have been and never can be expressed in any man-made hierarchy but which nevertheless are easily recognized by honest people. In any conversation between sensible people you will hear some persons referred to with deep respect and admiration, but others are dismissed with a shrug. The reason for such respect is never the position or the rank or the income of such persons but their personal qualities, their honesty, generosity, ability, in *whatever* work they do, or whatever position that occupy. They "have got something" and whatever they do, or say, their every word or action makes it known and inspires faith. These may be called carriers of the message of humanity. They are priests and ministers and bishops of the religion of every day life, whether they serve as nightwatchmen or as managing directors.

In the Armed Forces, the team spirit reaches its climax, particularly during action. Here also some prove to have an abundance of courage, generosity and faith, and they carry the others with them. They are found within all ranks, and form as it were, a hierarchy distinct and different from the ranks of officers and ratings. The decorations awarded for bravery and conscientious fulfillment of duty constitutes an effort to appreciate this particular hierarchy.

As in work or in military action, so there is a hierarchy of the spirit in the field of recreation, and these latter high priests are of no mean importance to the well-being and progress of man. Besides, with these many and various fields of human endeavor, the opportunity for leadership expands. A person maybe a total loss in the factory but the life of parties. Others excel at cards or in the bowling alley. Daydreamers and dramatuges are searching incessantly for all around heros and want to divide available heroism among a chosen few, leaving over just a mild contempt for the "masses," while the pleasant truth is that many if not most people are heroes in some way or other. The precious gems of heroism are more evenly distributed than moviemakers usually realize.

What is called recreation is just as important to man as that which is called "work." Together they fill the hours of his day and offer him his share of opportunities for learning and understanding life and for adopting a desired attitude toward it. Often the terms overlap. What is work to one maybe recreation to another. On the stage the actor is working while the spectator is enjoying his recreation. The work of the stars and directors of the screen is later reproduced for the entertainment of theatergoers. By paying actors for their work (and not always chicken feed either) the community shows that it considers their performance as much worthwhile as other paid work. No less important are amateur performances on improvised stages of our daily life—on bathing beaches, in wartime queues. All branches of art started with the amateurs who gave a fair abundance of the inspiration of the moment. Some of these might later to find that professional artists or players have honored them by swiping their "stuff." On the strength of such an encouragement, many an amateur has joined the ranks of professionals. Apart from such crafty climbing, the amateur performers spread the light of humor and wisdom on inconspicuous situations, turning trifling incidents into delight.

During the early part of the war, in London, the city of well-managed queues, a soldier from more rugged soil was pushing his way past the patiently waiting Britishers who gasped in horror at such indecorum, and a war within a war might easily have developed except for this cheerful remark by one who got pushed, "Leeway, folks, this gentleman appears to be in a hurry!" The soldier retreated.

During the last year of the German occupation of Norway when everybody talked about the coming German defeat and the lack of essential supplies within the German army, a couple of young Norwegians were stopped and searched by a Gestapo patrol on a street corner in Oslo. Such incidents were frequent and often led to bloody fights. Now one of the Norwegians remarked quietly, "What are you looking for anyway?"

"Arms!" barked a Gestapo man.

"Aw!" was the reply. "Haven't you even got them now!"

What is humor? To analyze it in all its aspects would be too bold a venture. Often it simply consists of discovering and demonstrating that a situation can be seen from a completely different angle than the usual one or the generally accepted one. This requires a keen and broad mind and often a generous heart. It may stop fights and also prevent wars. The playwrights, actors and humorists of every day life may be called the salt of the earth.

These heroes or leaders of everyday life operate through groups of humans, of which the smallest is the family, eventually extended to embrace servants and occasional guests. The highest enjoyments and the deepest despair are derived from family relations or conflicts and there is no subtler testing device for character than the family circle. The hierarchy of the spirit can also be found in most family groups, apart from the ancestral hierarchy. One of the parents, or children, or servants may have that blessed team spirit, that faith and generosity which polarizes the group and makes it a happy unity.

What about the others, the sad sacks who are non-entities in all fields, who are not overflowing with vitality, generosity or wisdom, whose minds are wobbling with worries over funds (or lack of such,) trouble with bosses (female or otherwise,) health, incompetence at work or horse-betting, who are tormented by a thousand itches? About these it has been said: "God must love them, since he made so many of them." Why does he make and love so many of these timid beings? We may be approaching the yardstick of God, which may be somewhat different from that of man! To him the conspicuous ones may not be so hot. He may be more happy with the plain and timid beings who examine and investigate for him the hard conditions through which they wade. Thus, even in the depths of his misery, the tired and beaten wanderer may be glad and proud to know that through his very hardships he offers to the cause of humanity a unique service which only he can perform. He may ask in despair, "Why am I unhappy? Was not everybody meant to be happy, and why did not the Creator make me so?" In due time he may arrive at some such answer: One may become happy at the end of the road and many times along the way but man was never promised by anyone to be continuously happy. The purpose of life is to gain experience and happiness is one of the baits. At a primitive stage, happiness is the reward of man's actions when he chooses rightly, as unhappiness is the result when he chooses wrongly. He is expected to choose wrongly quite a number of times and benefits by ensuing unhappiness—until he learns to choose rightly. And then—does he become eternally happy? No, at that time he has outgrown the chase for happiness. He is no longer a child in a ready-made universe governed by an all-powerful father. He is participating in the creation of the universe, which is not yet perfect. Viewed from infinity, God, the Creator, is all-powerful, but not within the time and space "He" has imposed upon himself. So, even when a man has learned to choose rightly, he will not necessarily be happy in the sense of being free from trouble. He can still be harmed by others and he will suffer under the strain of the Creative Artist who has not yet finished his job. But at this stage, he will not ask for happiness or worry over unhappiness. Those two words belong to his childish stage.

Both happiness and unhappiness, then, will follow man throughout all stages of his evolution, but the emphasis will change. His interest in either state will vanish as he grows in wisdom, character, honesty and selflessness.

Much unhappiness could be avoided for conscientious people if they would not insist on assuming a greater burden than they are able to carry. Athletes and circus artists overplay their acts, straining their muscles to fatigue, breaking their arms and legs and sometimes necks to please ferocious fans. Executives exhaust their brains and nerves in a hunt for quicker than necessary results, sometimes insisting upon doing themselves what their secretaries could have done better. But the most widespread overstrain is in the world of the emotions. We jump from the Empire State, the Golden Gate or selected spots in the Grand Canyon when we cannot "get" the woman we think we love. One even chained himself to a heated radiator until he was burned to death. When we do get the woman we think we love, and later find out we don't, there is the strain of remorse, self-pity, doubt and, eventually, the added burden of divorce courts, perjury, financial losses, and of seeing the look in the eyes of our children.

There is no greater scope than this for the science of vibration. It will not make men and women angels and wipe out divorces in a generation, but it may push us well along in this direction. Through this science it will be realized that there is more to marriage than a dazzling curl of hair and a tantalizing hip line. Armed with such knowledge, the stricken knight will be wary of making decisions until he has equated himself with a barrage of vibrations bursting from the maiden of his tentative choice. When this knowledge will have been established long enough to have developed into a social instinct, he will insist upon ample time for feeling and testing her vibratory assets before the final choice—and so will she. If she does not let him, he will shrug and give up the quest, knowing full well how unreliable was that first solitary whistle of his heart. If, on the other hand, he was so completely bowled over by this first look-see that he does chain himself to a heated radiator after all, then the better informed lady of his affections, rather than run to the press and report the thrilling news, will spend an afternoon with her overheated admirer, giving him gently a piece of her mind and of her vibrations in general, which may prove very different from that first hasty impression and thus sober him up. Finally, with a challenging word and a kiss of goodbye, she may make him cut his chains and go boldly out into the world in quest of new whirls.

Still, mistakes may happen. In spite of careful selection a married couple may someday feel a wall of chill rising between them. The rhythmic beats of one or both may have changed. The reason may be physical, such as excessive drinking. The cause may be freshly acquired mental or emotional impulses, such as new hobbies resulting in spending sprees or extracurricular heartbeats. There may be 1000 reasons, detected or undetected. Again, knowers of vibrations will have an advantage. They will proceed to change at an early stage, will feel no inclination to make scenes and will often be able to nip the trouble in the bud. If this be not possible, they will at least face the situation with fortitude. They know that the causes nearly always can be traced far back in their own or their ancestors' lives. They see this world of vibrations that started right back at the beginning of time, gradually leading up to this result. They have a better chance than others to find out where and how this current may be changed. They are able to except the inevitable cheerfully when it cannot be changed. The ignorant blames the other party. The half-informed blames himself. The well-informed blames no one. The ignorant wallows in self pity and will probably die early from high blood pressure. The half-informed tortures his mind with self-reproach and may lose his appetite and develop anemia. The well-informed treasures all experiences in his heart, which grows and blooms on this nutritious diet, making him finer, deeper, more broad-minded and generous after every new blow life has for him.

Right now Americans are being lectured and insulted from without and from within in regard to the high divorce rate. Although it took a graceful dip in 1947, it is still higher than in other countries. Few seem to realize the two main reasons: Americans can better afford it and, above all, marriage is taken more seriously in America than in any other country. Americans insist on being married to the girls they love, and will even go through the expense and agony of divorce to achieve this. In this sincerity lies a promise of a great future for the American family. The science of vibration has a chance of taking hold and growing in such an atmosphere of genuine intentions. Thus gradually the dreams and ideals of today may become realities of tomorrow. The high divorce rate of the present time, therefore, maybe considered a stepping stone from the hypocritical hollowness which is still prevailing in many countries—to the realization of our deepest yearnings.

Finally, what about that look in the children's eyes? Yes, it may be the thing that brings two erring parents back to love. If this cannot be achieved, then there is the next best course of honesty. How often parents underestimate their children's keen insight and make things worse by trying to "shield them" from the truth! Children may have tiny bodies and incomplete knowledge, but in detecting feelings and emotions they are quite often our betters. Also, they are equipped by nature to stand quite a bit of emotional strain. If they can be made to feel that both or at least one of the parents still love them, there is no end to what they can endure—and what help they can give! Their ambition is to live and serve in the world of adults. Instinctively, they know this is their goal. They are eager to see the world as it is and take a hand. But many parents treat them like personally-owned fragile china that must carefully be shielded from the knocks and blows of the world. Such were the ideas of the parents of India's Prince Gautama Buddha, who grew up in his palace knowing nothing of unhappiness, old age, sickness, poverty. When he finally walked out into the world and saw the grizzly truth, he became so shocked he retired to solitude and fasting. Later, again, he recovered and became a great teacher, so in the end he became useful after all. But modern American parents would not want their children to retire to the Grand Canyon or the Oceano dunes and live on a cup of rice a day – even for a period of recovery from shock! They want them to go straight into business and make good. They want them to marry and be happy. There can be no better way toward this goal than letting them share in life as it is, smooth or tough. Apart from that, the atmosphere in the home of disharmony may mean worse suffering to a sensitive child than seeing his parents separated.

Again, the science of vibration could save us from exaggerated notions of parental responsibilities. Parenthood is a trusteeship employing a limited scope of responsibility for a limited duration of time. Besides the influence of school, community and the whole thumping, searching life around, below and above him, the child has his parents to turn to for friendship, support, love and advice. Often parents do more good by what they don't do that what they do. One thoughtful father described his duties thus: living his own life as truthfully as he can, letting the children share in it uncompromisingly.

As, by and by, our world of vibrations will yield its secrets, we may thus acquire a new measuring rod with which to gauge our future husband or wife or child or friend, and also a magic wand with which to "still the storm" if such there be. We will know the latent powers hidden in man, And if in some cases, these powers should happen to be too well hidden, we may call them forth as easily as we now put on a collar and tie–those cute inventions which the male hero of our species briefly puts around his neck like a hangman's noose.

One, who had made vibration his creed, used to say: "My attitude to any man I meet I consider my attitude to God, and any man's attitude to me I see as God's attitude!"

He saw the surging vibrations of the universe approaching him in any man. But suppose the one we thus honor is a burglar whom we hear rummaging around in our basement? Should we consider him, too, a representative of The ONE, not to be interfered with? If he is representative so is the policeman and the district attorney. All three are different aspects or evolutionary stages of the Universal Spirit battling out between them a great problem of future evolution and "whither man?" Many factors beyond his reach may have made this man a burglar, and we may refuse to pass moral judgment on him, but to live and evolve in a community, the others must have order. We have a right and duty to protect ourselves—against individual offenders as well as against offending nations.

In connection with the notion of protection, however, many people insist on the principle of punishment. Do these two go well together? Can they be served efficiently by the same institutions? The term punishment in modern thinking and law is adorned with all sorts of high motives, including education and restoration. But studying human history, it is evident that punishment is a family relation of revenge and can never be completely detached from that sentiment. At an earlier age, revenge may have been a proper thing. But when a wise man of yore said "Let him throw the first stone who is without guilt"–he meant to evoke a new and truer kind of sentiment in man. Well, who wants to throw that stone?

Institutions and procedures established according to the pure motive and system of protection would probably be cheaper, and certainly more efficient. They would also better serve the education of the criminal. Under existing conditions, for instance, a thief or forger may get a short jail term, then come out and repeat his crime gleefully. Under an efficient protective system, the thief or forger would be barred from any public or private position in which he could repeat his folly, as long as psychiatrists considered him not cured of his mental disease. The psychiatrist might be wrong in some cases, but this procedure at least attacks the problem squarely, employing our available knowledge in solving it. Under present conditions, even one who has murdered or tortured others for simple gain or perverted pleasure, may be released and get a chance again to indulge in his immature pastime when his time has been served and irrespective of the state of his mind. Under a protective system, such a person would not be allowed to move about freely until several independent psychiatrists would have agreed he had been cured. Apart from that, his life would be made as useful and as pleasant as possible. For a thief to be excluded from responsible positions and from any activity permitting him to steal as long as he remained, mentally, a thief, and for a murderer to be isolated from society as long as he remained a murderer, would be a stronger deterrent to the criminal than the prospect of a few years in jail, depending somewhat on the good graces of a judge! Above all, it would take glamour off crime and make it appear as what it really is: a disease.

Even at present criminals are diagnosed by psychiatrists, but this is done chiefly to determine whether they are fit for trial, or to furnish material for the defense. Not until medical science and institutions have replaced all courts, trials and jails can we have anything in the way of a scientific approach to crime diseases. Such a development would be particularly important in the case of international criminals such as the top Nazis, and the Japanese warlords who had held important positions in government and private business, which would indicate they represented common trends. Such a procedure would be more humiliating than any punishment in the ordinary sense, stripping the criminal more completely of glory. This may be a comforting thought to those who cannot get rid of their punishment complex. Becoming guinea pigs of science would make the criminals useful to humanity and repay some of the heavy debt they owe. Under the present system, on top of the debt they owe already, they are marched as dark heroes through court procedures, wasting the time of high-salaried lawyers, generals, witnesses, newspapermen and commentators, all of whom, along with the reading public, could and should have used that time for essential work in building up our future instead of tying down our minds and emotions to lurid backslidings.

Well-intentioned schemes for education of criminals are often wasted at the present because available scientific knowledge is not applied. Every school teacher knows the difficulty of teaching children of vastly different minds, temperaments or inclinations the same things in the same classes. This problem is intensified in prisons, whose inmates range from the very lowest to the highest intelligence grades and include all age groups. In addition, there are the special ailments that made them criminals, and no education will do unless blended with psychological treatment of these ailments. The safest and most important aspect of education is, as always, education of normal children—to prevent them from becoming criminals.

In trying to disconnect the thoughts of revenge from our treatment of crime, the hardest case to deal with is torture. How can we look without passion at people who have tortured helpless prisoners or given orders to do so? Accordingly, they are sentenced to death, and even that is considered too mild. How can we tell whether it is mild or severe? What do we know of death? We know something of the reactions to this sentence, before the execution takes place. We know that many hardened and heartless criminals have no fear of death, so the sentence appears to be inadequate as a punishment! Others become insane from fear. These facts should be sufficient to condemn the death sentence as either a means of punishment or a treatment of criminals. The executed criminal is forever removed from our sphere of examination. No new advances in science can be tried on him. Should he ever be proven innocent, there is no going back on the deal. And what about the hereafter? We are sending the criminal—or the wrongly sentenced suspect—to a world of which we have no knowledge. It may be worse than this one, or better. We may be doing our man a fateful injustice—or a great favor. We are, in fact, meddling in things and worlds that are not our business.

As long as our man remains in this world, he will at least have a chance to suffer the consequences of his deeds, or be rehabilitated if unjustly sentenced. Some of the torturers of the last war period, particularly Germans, have been overtaken by a mental punishment which they insist is worse than physical tortures of their wildest imagination. They have been heard to scream that they were willing to suffer all the agonies of their victims rather than that which they went through. Something caught up with them and make them victims of the law of cause and effect with which they have played so carelessly. There were other such criminals, Japanese and Germans, who proudly posed before photographers in Tokyo or at the glamour show in Nürnberg, apparently without any feeling of regret. How easily we let them off by sending them over the line in that state of mind, before they had time to study the thought-provoking pictures of their own crimes in their cells or at the working places!

An increasing number of otherwise helpful and conscientious citizens try consistently to escape jury service. If they cannot wiggle out of it, they refuse to say the little word "guilty" even if guilt is beyond doubt. Why? Because, they say, they won't assist in taking life. They feel that, from whatever angle they look at it, the death sentence is inadequate. It provides neither punishment nor education of the criminal, does not furnish the community with information that will help combat crime and is no expression of justice. Even the protection of the community can now be achieved as effectively or more effectively by other means. Crime has decreased wherever the death sentence has been abolished as seen in eight of the United States, in Scandinavia and in Switzerland. In England, crime decreased radically when the number of criminal offenses punishable by death was reduced from 200 to 1.

The reason seems to be that abolishment of the death sentence tones down the sensation around crime. This improves the mental and emotional health of the public.

Once the criminal has been committed to protective custody, medical examinations and useful work, any further cravings for punishment appears to be a debasing waste of emotional energy, a sign of mental feebleness, retarding progress. The healthy man would save his steam for better purposes. The past he cannot change; the promised land is in the future. Of that he is master if he so wishes. This future has plenty of vital questions awaiting his decision. How will the changes ahead affect his own job and his sons? How will he adjust income and buying power to the great amount of production which is already possible here –and to the still larger scale which will be realized with atomic power in industry and other new inventions? He is not called upon to solve the riddle. Several alternative solutions have already been hatched by experts. The only thing he is asked to do is occupy his mind with such topics, studying as far as his time permits, or at least be interested in them. In due time the decision will be up to him. While this has been neglected by nearly everybody except a few experts and heretics, the international situation, on the other hand, has been spotlighted by a barrage of propaganda and ideas from an endless chain of organizations. But he has heard little of the foundation for international relations, such as trade and finance. In these fields too, his decisions will make or mar our world.

The advent of atomic energy has hastened the pace but not fundamentally changed the picture. This advent could have been retarded but not avoided. At the turn-of-the-century the crucial discoveries that led to atom splitting were made–

simultaneously in many countries and were natural sequences to earlier research. Yet, if man be seen as the instrument, the assistant and even the expression of God, it would not be wrong to say, as religious people do, that atomic power is a method used by the Creator to prompt man to more rapid spiritual progress. A revelation through physical science has become a spur to cooperation and a broader and more sincere outlook—as happened before, and will happen again. Is man ready for this tremendous power? There is no reason why he should be. Man was never ready for the conditions into which he was placed, but these conditions helped him to grow up to them. Not realizing this, people sometimes refuse heroically to take part in any work or reform projects for their community, insisting that they must reform themselves first. Evidently they have some idea about becoming perfect and then going to work. It would take a long time to become perfect in this way and the community would have to wait even longer. On the other hand, he who sees the community and its members as one interwoven system of vibrations does not worry much about when or where or how to start work. All work for his community is to his view simultaneously changing and reforming himself, and every bit of work on his own mind and character he sees reflected in the state of his community. In the balance between these mutual influences, he perceives the art of life and the secret of attainment.

CHAPTER 6

THE FAMILY OF NATIONS

The sweetness of family life is often peppered, so it is no mockery to speak about "a family of nations." The important thing about a family is not its proverbial happiness, but its *purpose*. A family is an association of unequals. Towards the international family we piously close our eyes, pretending nations are equals. In the family circle the different ages of the members keep them constantly reminded of their inequality. Tolerance, patience, helpfulness frequently result. In the circle of nations the inequality is not always so obvious.

Family members do not come to the breakfast table to make clever deals, to preach sermons. They come to eat breakfast. In addition, a father may give helpful advice, a mother loving care, and a son may stretch and assert himself without running the risk of an atom war. He may later become stronger and brighter than his dad without bragging about it.

The family is the factory and testing ground for character, where rugged individualists learn their first and also last lesson of community life. The family of nations is a wider testing ground.

It took a long time before the principles of the family circle were extended to larger communities and finally, to the whole nation. There was a time when well-behaved people would not interfere, whatever appeared to happen within the house of a stranger. In some countries this is still so. But in what we call civilized nations, cries for help from a stranger's house, for example, would not go unheeded today. People in their right mind would break into such a house if they thought it necessary. The sense of solidarity is stronger than fear of trouble.

In the international field cries for help may still go unheeded. Many close their ears, particularly if they are not too near the scenes of horror—and dream about peace by non-interference and disarmament.

Kurt Breier cannot do that. He is a taxi driver in Baden Baden, the capital of the French zone of Germany. He was on the Eastern front, became a prisoner of the Russians, was freed and sent to the British zone of Germany, then to the American zone and finally to his native Baden-Baden in the French zone. Like many of his countrymen he has felt the yoke of four foreign powers and has a grim and cynical concept of the "family of nations."

"But we get along with the French now," he told me, while driving to the deep forests of Schwarzwald in April, 1949. "One month's gasoline ration would not reach for this single trip," he added, "but the French are practical. They make concessions—and a little profit on the side. Not so the Americans, or the British."

"And the Russians?"

"I am glad their women are not with us," replied Kurt. "When do we start the war against them?" Then he told me unprintable stories of Russian women on the Eastern front. His stories were in stark contrast to my own experiences. I had been with the Russian army in the far north for months, in Russia proper and in the Norwegian Port Kirkenes. The Russian soldiers let the Norwegians entirely alone. There were many Russian women with the soldiers— lithe, wide-eyed girls, some of them very pretty. They gathered in their own messes, singing, dancing. Often Norwegians were invited, but I never saw or heard of any unfortunate incident.

I had been to southern Russia as a civilian and had grateful recollections of the friendliness and helpfulness of Southern Russians.

Yet, Kurt's stories about Russian cruelty were hardly without foundation. There are too many such stories. But Kurt had been a German soldier, part of an army that murdered and burned its way across the Russian steppes.

The Russian soldiers in Kirkenes knew that Norwegians had practically saved the lives of 100,000 Russians who were kept in Norway by the Nazis as prisoners of war. Braving the threats of death and torture, Norwegians had given these Russians food and blankets, and hidden them when they escaped. The Russians remembered, and showed their gratitude. They proved that they were not cruel by nature.

Despite such incidents of mutual friendship, grave suspicion today separates the Soviet Bloc from the rest of the world. Rumors of war fly as sparks from this high power extension. What is behind it? Hard realities or mere misunderstandings?

Both. The misunderstanding may be disposed of first—the conflict is between capitalism and communism, say some. Capitalism means simply accumulation of means of production and transportation for efficient producing and distributing. The Russian five year plans were demonstrations of capitalism on a colossal scale. Some might object that capitalism implies private ownership of the means of production, as contrasted with government ownership. In the Soviet factories the directors and governmental agencies have greater personal power than most leaders of American factories, and their proportion of the income is also relatively greater than the profit-plus-management salaries in most American enterprises. Thus, it is hard to find ideological difference.

Communism on the other hand, meant originally a feeling of oneness, a sense of cooperation which, perhaps, was stronger among the American pioneers than in any other group of people, including the present Soviet community. Communism as a set of rules or laws for communist parties is of course another matter. Thus, the terms are ambiguous, but referring to their original sense one may say that all modern societies must contain both capitalism and communism in order to function properly. And inherent "conflict" between these two concepts is an absurdity.

Equally confusing is the talk about a breach between East and West. It is particularly curious that such ideas can take hold in America, where people from both East and West and all other global directions met and intermarried and formed one nation. No east or west or north or south have ever determined human character or behavior. The most typical Eastern country–India–is closer to the United States than to Russia in ideology and purpose.

Finally, there is the belief that unbridgeable differences exist between the people of the Soviet Bloc and other people. This may appear so on the surface, when one considers the discussions in the United Nations and other organizations where only officials of nations speak. Not long ago, however, other officials spoke for many of the nations now within the Soviet Bloc and their language was not difficult to understand. Those who can remember the old League of Nations may also recall a Soviet official who could make himself very clearly understood to our simple western minds–Maxim Livinov.

This brings us toward the core of the problem.

Wise, gray-haired madam Joliot-Curie, daughter of the inventor of radium and a sincere friend of Russia, sat back in her laboratory chair at Rue11 Pierre Curie in Paris, April 25, 1949.

"Even my husband and I have very little contact with Russia now," she told me. "It appears the Russians are afraid. For one thing they are afraid of the atom bomb, against which there is no defense–but secrecy! Their only possible hope, in case of war, is that nobody knows where their vital establishments and transportation centers are."

No doubt many Russians are afraid of the atom bomb, though their responsible leaders hardly believe America will attack. But they have other fears.

In the summer of 1927 I found myself stranded in Odessa, without funds. I was a nondescript tourist without any political affiliation, on no official mission. Odessa, the principal Russian city in the south, it is called the pearl of the Black Sea. To me it proved a pearl indeed. I was adopted by a group of students who were studying to become merchant marine officers. They lived in an old palace on the outskirts of town. I tried to put up my tent in their garden. When they learned about my plight, they conducted me in triumph to their quarters. They took one blanket from each of their own beds until I had 20 blankets to cover my humble self. Their offerings of food were equally magnanimous. And the secret police agents of the locality? They had their hands full cabling Moscow and cutting red tape to make my stay a legal triumph!

Such was the Russian spirit in 1927.

I found the same catching friendliness and boundless hospitality among the Russian soldiers in the far north in 1945. I heard them sing with the same buoyant voices. They were the same people. But there was a clear tremor in their melancholy songs, a nervous twitch in their faces. What had happened?

There are reports which cannot be ignored.

April 30, 1949, New York morning papers had a third installment of Col. James C Crockett's recollections from his stay in Moscow as US military attaché. He wrote about an incident he witnessed recently outside the Grand Hotel Restaurant in Moscow. A boy, obviously drunk, tried to enter the restaurant, which was reserved for foreigners and selected Russians. He lurched forward, seizing the doorknob after secret police agent had told him he could not enter. Two police agents grabbed him by the arms, hauled him to the edge of the sidewalk. One twisted his arm behind his back, pulled it until it broke, then knocked him down. The other kicked him into the gutter.

Around the corner people were grunting and spitting in

the street as an expression of indignation. But no one dared help the boy or complain about the police.

As an isolated incident this might have happened in America, England, anywhere. Col. Crockett wrote however, that "such brutality... is unceasing within the Soviet Union today." If this be true, what is the reason? What has happened in Russia? A Polish veterinarian who arrived in the United States in March, 1949, said the Russians had forced him to act as a doctor for the soldiers. During his time with the army he saw Ukrainian farmers who had been unwilling to join the Cooperative Farms fenced in behind barbed wire and starved to death while officers told the soldiers to eat the food they had taken from these farmers before their eyes. Finally the starving farmers began killing each other.

There have been widely divergent rumors about the number of Russians in concentration camps. December 27, 1948, an official American estimate was given for the first time. Army Sec. Kenneth Royal said at a press conference in Berlin that the number was 13 million. Earlier, Alexandre Kerensky, the revolutionary leader who freed the Russians from Lazar, had estimated the number at 12 million.

If Kenneth Royal's figures are correct, how can they be explained? Why are more than 6% of the Russian people behind barbed wire? Why is the relation between the people and its police officials highlighted by incidents of maddening brutality?

The Russian people have had secret police since the time of Peter the Great. This would explain the existence of a secret police today, but not the brutality, nor the unequal number of prisoners. Why the difference between Russia today and in 1927?

The only explanation is that the present leaders are desperate, cringing with fear. Their fear is not a foreign power, an atom bomb or an Atlantic Pact. Their maddening fear is, primarily, of their own people. This fear and desperation within spreads as a disease and manifests, secondarily, as fear and instability in the international field. Grabbing of more territory—by any means short of war—becomes the necessity for bolstering up the homefront and the morale.

A distinguished councillor of the Cour des Comptes in Paris, told me in the early summer of 1949 that according to dependable estimates 500 Red Army officers had deserted in the course of the past month. The number of deserting enlisted men had not even been counted. For obvious reasons these figures do not usually reach the press, so American papers have had detailed reports of several desertions by Russian aviators lately.

"French intelligence estimates," said my source, "that Russia cannot go to war for at least 20 years. The present generation has no stomach for marching. Only a new generation can be persuaded to do so."

French intelligence maybe wrong. But there is a solid body of information behind its estimate.

The firing of Dr. Piotr Kapitza, Russian atom scientist, in September 1948, along with later incidents, indicate the Russians have no atom bomb. They have possibly other weapons, such as a ray that can stop engines, a sound gun, germs and new gases. But they have neither the necessary means of transportation nor the stomach to conduct a major war.

This, however, does not dispose of the explosive tension between the people of the Soviet Bloc and its leaders. It is a sickening fever affecting all nations. The solution is up to humanity as a whole. Its success or failure will be a test of our maturity.

The first step is to gather definite information. It may be difficult for a single nation, for example America, to ask Russia about its police and concentration camps. The answer might be a counter question about American justice in poll tax states. Any one nation has weaknesses that makes it difficult for it to assume the position of a moral judge, though its sins may be on a relatively small scale. Even at this stage we discover the need for federation. A federation of all or most nations has the right to ask questions and the power to obtain a reply. It is significant that the first official discussion of Russian concentration camps was brought up at the October, 1948, session of the United Nations— our present feeler toward world federation. If this beginning will lead to definite results, the United Nations will have proven its worth.

Other less extensive but more concrete expressions of Federation are the Atlantic Pact—and its earlier sister organization, the Soviet Bloc. The very existence of these two federations is pressing for an answer to the above question.

Our present information about Soviet concentration camps, however incomplete as yet, is formidable enough to enable us to pose the next question: what has caused this despair and fear on the part of Soviet leaders?

Partly a sincere disappointment. Many of these leaders believed honestly in Karl Marx and his concept of man and evolution. The Russian people accepted gladly industrialization, education and a general progress, but not the involved Marxist doctrines. This stirred the fanatics to ever more brutality. Now there is a maddening race with time. The harassed augurs waiver between complete desperation and a faint hope that if they increase the terror just a little bit, they will get over the hump and into the normal evolutionary pattern that Marx promised.

When the economic doctrines of Robert Owen, St. Simon and Proudhon (once known as Socialism) were polluted by the odd Hegelian philosopher, Karl Marx, nobody probably dreamt that this would split up the labor movement of the world into squabbling sects and contribute to the inhuman torture of millions of human beings!

Many of us have sniffed at the voluminous works of Marx but it has been reported that five persons actually have perused them in their entirety. Two of these got incurable insomnia—so the story goes—one became a convinced Marxist, and the remaining two were fortunate enough to go crazy, thus being relieved of any further conscious sufferings.

When people become desperate, verbal persuasion will hardly affect them, but solid facts may. The Soviet leaders are sufficiently realistic to yield to facts, and to action. Proper action may bring results that could not be reached through negotiations.

The purpose of such action would be first to create a source of power—not primarily physical power, but, above all, moral power. Next, this organ of power must clearly define its purpose and state its wishes.

The source of power would be the Federation.

The pattern for this is the atom, the smallest world we know. The atom is a Federation within which electrons, neutrons, positrons, mesons and other citizens and soldiers work and play and keep their powder dry, baffling with tremendous force would-be intruders. In the atom there never was a disarmament campaign! There is constant vigilance, uninterrupted preparedness. But it does happen that intruding forces are strong enough to cross the border and conquer. Cosmic rays have done so for longer than we can remember. Recently man has made his own cosmic rays, produced in the synchrotron—a bigger and better cyclotron—and reaching about 1 billionth the strength of real cosmic rays. During production of atom bombs, also, man leads invading forces into the atom.

Through this display of power the universe unfolds and reaches its purpose. Is man above, beneath or beyond this universe—or solidly planted inside it? In the latter case, should he not take a cue from the atom, that his destination is not to relinquish power, but increases it—and use it? In using it, he develops a sense of right or wrong. This sense has not matured yet. Man does not today agree on what is right or wrong. But little by little patterns are forming which are accepted by increasing numbers. This finds expression in Federation.

Federation is not reached through disarmament but through stronger-than-ever armament of the units that want to federate. Power must be increased, not abolished.

Federation will not mean peace in any absolute sense. It will mean reduction of international war to the battles between the federated police forces and any intruder nations or groups. This will mean reduction, though not an elimination, of bloodshed; reasonable freedom for more people, though not unlimited freedom for anybody; greater efficiency, though not perfection. The choice is hardly ever between good or evil, perfect or imperfect, but between better and worse.

Evolution has constantly been working toward this end. From the Babylonian to the Persian, Greek and Roman era, progress (with setbacks) was achieved from wild, uncontrolled, "evil" design to more orderly, efficient, "human," or "good" vibrations. The Old Testament dramatizes the struggle between Egyptian disruptive brutality and Hebrew unity and humanity. In the New Testament this trend is crystallized in the message and person of the Messiah, who was not a unique freak of nature but an anticipation of a mature and normal man. In modern times the League of Nations and later again the United Nations and the Atlantic Pact were steps on the same ladder.

Similarly, Federal Union, Citizens Committee for United Nations Reform and World Federalists are expressions of a definite wish among the people of America and many other nations to make this globe a cooperative unit based on free will.

The present most concrete expression of federation, the Atlantic Pact, represents already such an overwhelming power that it is quite unnecessary for this group to shake its club. On the other hand, it is high time for it to show its purpose and wishes—in action. The objective of a federation, obviously, is not only to promote peace but also—freedom from want.

There is "want" in many areas in the world today, for example, obviously within the Soviet Bloc, particularly among the children. They lack proper shelter, medical care, vitamins, clothing. If there could be assurance that the help would reach the really needy, large amounts could be collected by private appeal. America and the Atlantic Pact nations live in the spirit of giving and are constantly seeking outlet for this urge.

If such aid were collected and the Soviet government were approached without any special preparation, they might well turn down the gifts, in line with earlier policy, and either not inform the Russian people at all, or give a distorted version of the story. The case would be entirely different if the Russian masses were informed, in advance. There are, even now, various and extensive underground channels by which news is carried into and out of Russia. These channels could be used and new ones established. By radio, leaflets, coded letters and word-of-mouth the Russian people could be duly informed about the gifts collected for them, about the scope and purpose of the Atlantic Pact.

Then the official offer could be transmitted to the Soviet government. Would Soviet leaders dare turn down such an offer, with their people being already informed? If they did, this might mean their undoing. This might be the last straw that would release an avalanche to which the nations of the Atlantic Pact could not be passive onlookers.

Most probably, however, the Soviet leaders would accept the gifts and face the facts. The gifts would be brought by agents of the givers. Exchange of information and news would again be established. The tension within the Soviet orbit would gradually evaporate. The Soviet leaders might finally realize that it cost too much trying to hide facts—however discouraging some of these facts might appear. Once the news exchange became free, the West might prove to have a greater understanding even of the unpleasant facts than Soviet leaders suspected. There are individuals who feel so different that they have an urge to hide. Psychology calls this a mental quirk. It is no less a quirk when applied to nations.

But as long as we have not offered genuine aid to Russian children, we others have little right to criticize. It has been said the starvation of German children in 1919-1923, after the first World War, laid the foundation for World War II, 20 years later. Can we afford to risk a third World War 20 years from now?

Reduction of the tension within the Soviet Bloc would change the entire international picture. But even now, today, some temporary solution could be found, or at least tried, for example in Germany. The whole of Europe is suffering because of the German situation, the almost impassable dividing line separating East and West. When Russia blockaded Berlin, the airlift was a great technical and tactical victory for the West, but the strategic vision appears to have been lacking.

Among others, Maurice Duverger pointed out in *Le Monde* (Paris, 11 April, 1949) that no sincere effort had until then been made to reach a satisfactory solution. By retiring all troops, Germany could be made a buffer state. In detail his proposition was not quite clear. He seemed to want to remove all control. A practical solution would be civilian inspectors recruited from all four occupying powers, and working together as they do, for example, in Austria.

Before the Atlantic Pact had been realized it was conceivable that Russia might have opposed such a course. Today she would have to go along—if the West insisted. The plan would put all the occupying powers at the same advantage—or disadvantage. No one would lose face. The inspection could be at least as effective as it is now. There would be no competitive bids from East or West. Germany would have less chance of rearming than she has at present, with her Russian sponsored "police forces" which could eventually be converted into a proper German army.

As for winning over the German people, Americans have a better chance from across the Rhine, particularly if we will drop our coy pretense of being just tough guys with the exclusive ambition of making money and getting ahead.

Could we overcome our shyness for the sake of world understanding? Could we take the pioneer ideals (which still are the power behind our lives) out of the sacred closets, dust them off and streamline them and show them forth while blushing humbly in the knowledge of how far we still are from the goal? Rigid economic and political doctrines born of poverty are not fought merely by saying "we have more tractors." We must also know and tell why. We have more tractors because cooperation worked better than class struggle, equality of opportunity made us richer than the equality of marionettes, government by ballot proved more efficient than by dictate.

Europe is tired of extremist ideologies that wrecked it and is wide open for the new or old line which America tried.

Asia may be even more responsive, and is also the greater price. The aid to China's Chang Kai-shek, most of which is reported to have fallen into Communist hands, provided a precious lesson for future engagements. The America that Asia wants and admires is crusading America, the America that rose against British domination, that invited peoples of all creeds and nations to become citizens, the America that fought a bloody Civil War to free slaves, the America that beat down tyrants and exploiters. If America will seek out and cooperate with people of this spirit and sentiment in Asia, then East and West shall meet.

Within the Eastern nations with their memorable past many tend to look back—and even turn back—to what appears to them the peak of existence. But it was said in the Old Testament that the wife of Lot turned into a pillar of salt because she looked back. Who wants to become a pillar of salt?

The late Mahondas Gandhi and his spinning wheel have still a strong hold on some Hindu minds. They turn their backs on modern industry.

Industry and science were the reward to man for his courageous quest to conquer matter. But mass production changed his social life. Many of the rules and customs of the earlier society became obsolete. He had to start from scratch in the social world again, uncouth and ill-mannered. It will take time to acquire the niceties and grace of the best medieval knights or ancient kings, but when he does he will do better than the knights, for he will have more to offer. Whatever the price, whatever the delay, the road to material and spiritual freedom obviously goes through science and industry which will give to the individuals within all nations, in their own good time, a measure of economic independence and liberty that will release their power for broad and wide thinking, the very requisite for real freedom.

Industry and business are radiations resulting from fusion of mind and matter. Human thoughts bombarded the world of matter like electrons bombarding uranium atoms. This caused chain reactions named industry and business. It is up to us to direct and exploit this process, but trying to stop or reverse it would be as futile as trying to stop evolution. Industry and business are irrevocably linked to the future of the family of nations.

Some confine industry and business by the term materialism as contrasted to spirituality, by which they sometimes mean meditating in mountain caves or starving themselves in jail. But all their meditation or starvation cannot help one starving Hindu fill his stomach or his mind. Industry on the other hand, feeds the bodies so the minds can reach the goal of their ambitions. Industry springs from spirituality and also sustains it. Meditation is a luxury of spirituality. It may be enjoyed or abused.

Even if man has sufficient skill and drive to industrialize the whole world could our resources sustain such expansion?

Wild guesses, exaggerations, understatement have cluttered this question but in the 1920s an inventory of American resources was started, under the direction of Herbert Hoover. This was later supplemented by careful estimates for the rest of the world. From these sources, we know, for example, that food production could be raised much faster than population could increase, provided our knowledge of the soil conservation, factory farms and new processes for fertilizer production be properly utilized. In addition there are vast untapped resources of the oceans. Large oil supplies have recently been discovered under ocean bottoms near the United States. These supplies would at least keep us happy until synthetic oil and atomic power would be flowing. All items that are now short can be replaced by others equally well suited for the purpose, and of this chain of supplies there is no end in view. As long as present scientific knowledge, industrial skills, ambitions and working hours are maintained, the entire humanity may gradually be raised to a healthful living standard and enjoy this standard without interruption.

However, this requires some degree of international cooperation. Even the United States, the most self-sufficient of all nations, needs some imports. For example, Russia provides the United States with ingredients for steel alloys used in armor plate. This side of the picture has to be remembered by those concerned with US exports to Russia. No nation is self-sufficient. This fact irks political dreamers who try to change it by aggression, through ruse or war. Mature statesmen reason the other way: if nations are not self-sufficient, if only to trade, then trade there must be. Even if one single nation might achieve self-sufficiency, that would not change the world picture. Such a nation would not live very happily in a world of traders. Successful statesmen considered their nation's interests along with the world's, while those who planned their nation's course against the interests of the rest of the world found or will find they planned in vain.

While no one can claim the world as his ally, one may try

to find its side. It is the trying that matters. In trying sincerely to discern the way of evolution, the road of the future, the hope and gropings of the world, the seeker will sharpen his judgment and come closer to his goal and his nation's goal.

The play of nations, like family life, is a game in which man learns to play fair or foul. The rise and decay of nations has no other purpose than education of man. The importance of this game lies in the importance of human character. For this prize package of nature, wars have been fought and through its achievement, peace may be gained. But peace is no primary goal and will not come about except as a result of character maturity. As long as grave injustice is being done and human beings are intimidated– anywhere–men will go to war if other means do not produce results. To obtain peace, one must work for justice first.

Has human character now reached such average maturity that we are ready for world federation? Soundings through the United Nations and other organizations indicate three quarters of the globe's population want to federate now. Such a step would not only promote international peace. When estimated world resources as mentioned above, would be properly exploited by global federation, this would raise living standards to new peaks, but would also incur new hardships. Unemployment would be overcome, all willing hands could be offered remunerative work–of some kind. Nobody would need to starve. On the other hand, nobody could be sure of keeping the job he had, in the place where he used to live. The closer international cooperation would result in switching whole industries, concentrating each kind in the best suited areas. The rapid progress would favor prompt establishment of new industries and prompt abandonment of obsolete ones.

However, change of job and environment are gains, not hardships, from the point of view of character training and education, particularly when coupled with higher living standards, more leisure and more opportunity to enjoy it. In a cooperative world, change of job would, on the average, mean more income. Community life would be so organized that family raising would no more involve economic handicap for anybody.

Not only does history show a gradual evolution toward world federation, but there have been definite feelings and forerunners. Switzerland has been a small federation of cantons for centuries. The British Empire was a large federation granting nearly equal rights with the Mother Country to the "Dominions" (Canada, South Africa, Australia etc.) while the "Crown Colonies" were more in the nature of possessions, in style with older empires. As a whole, the British Empire marked a step forward toward the principle of federation. The next step was taken by the United States, the first true pattern of a world federation of nations.

In *Flowering Dusk* (Longmans Green, 1945) Ella Young, Irish poetess, writes:

How could I know, America,
Hearing you praised for bigness,
For opulence alone,
As a calf is praised for the market,
How could I know you a land
Lean-ribbed and austere,
Splendid as a lioness
Golden-eyed and langourously alert?

America, lioness, langourously alert, was the first British colony to shake her shackles, impatiently reaching for freedom—and for the next step in world organization. America was the first to accept as citizens men of any creed or race, to form a nation based on *ideas* rather than blood and soil. She was the first to fight for colored men. Today she is the lioness and herald of the world federation based on her own pattern.

The rugged Empire that once was her chastising father is now trudging along, close on her heels, bruised and shaken, but determined. Old man Britain did not always extend his domain by the gentle touch of silken gloves, but he has risen with the rising tide and read the signs of the times. He has proven his faith in federation by freeing his most precious possession, India, the mainstay of his empire.

Independent India has become an instrument and testing ground of federation. From being a British possession, it has become a link between America and Great Britain bound to the latter by custom and momentum but to the former by need and similarity of spirit. America is the only nation that can help India industrialize and overcome starvation. America and India share their spiritual independence, with the difference that America succeeded first, India later, through American inspiration. America and India both wished to federate their various states. America succeeded and through her success inspired India. In return for such practical aid, India's deep treasures may charm and enlighten the world after they have been revitalized by the fresh winds of critical research.

Neighboring China is a slippery prize but could be won for western federation if her wholesome men be supported who, like the ancient mandarins, humbly live and breathe in their nation's past and future without bragging about either. If her present inner struggle is to shed parasites and bring gold to the fore, outside support must be in the right place —or not at all. Then these "sons and daughters of Heaven" could also become children of the earth.

Watching all is a giant bear, clutching Asia and Europe, rocking menacingly. While the bear is the symbol of its strength, its soul is like an orchestra with a woman conductor, sensitive of heart, fiery of temperament. Its emotions and thoughts cover the widest scales, its writers and poets reach the peak of visionaries. Generously but recklessly it experimented with itself, cutting big slices of its flesh in the process, so those who know and love this nation of too bold adventurers cover their eyes in despair. When the storm of its soul will have spent its fury and left wisdom in its wake, it will reach its peak of graceful power. Before such attainment, wild ambitions must be curbed, rigid viewpoints of its clique of leaders must be softened and adapted to the universal radiations of love, unless this giant nation shall perish, like others have, and mar the world by its death struggle.

The world of man, like that of matter, marches ahead and reaches new goals by battles and explosions or through subtle infiltration and radiation. Viewed from eternity, our present concern is trivial. Whether we reach our next stage on the ladder of evolution by peaceful federation or through an atom war may merely be a matter of 1000 years or so— an eyewink in the ages of history.

However, we are blessed with the power of narrowing our view and looking at things in terms of our present lives. From this narrow point of view we would prefer to advance the smoother way, and so we may. In the press and over the air, in colleges, in Congress, in United Nations sessions, a thought is taking hold, a concept is forged: federation. One government for all the world, starting with those nations who already want to go ahead.

If three quarters of the world's population want federation now, as various soundings indicate, then there is sufficient foundation for immediate action. There is also an instrument ready. The United Nations may not be a world power yet, but it is a suitable organization through which to take preliminary steps. Through the United Nations, member nations could propose and establish a world government with armed police. Or a world federation could grow out of the present Atlantic Pact. Or from the Soviet point of view, world federation may grow out of the present Soviet Bloc. The winner will be the one who can make the most genuine appeal. Conceit or trickery will not go far. So the competition between various groups for the prize that is the world is favorable to progress. Each side will have to do its utmost and be on its best behavior. We have a war going on right now, a war in which the weapons are, or will be, fairness, generosity, cooperative spirit. The globe is the price.

When the winner emerges, will he have difficulty collecting the stakes?

Not much, although there may be delays. One or two or even 10 nations temporarily remaining outside a world federation could never constitute a serious threat to the latter, either physically or economically. All the disadvantages would be on the side of the outside nations who would be entirely at the mercy of the federation. The latter could, if it so chose, set up rules for international relations, trade, treatment of subjects, and enforce such rules inside and outside its orbit. For all practical purposes the whole world would be federated already, and the outside nations could do no better than joining.

At Wolfshagen near Gosselaar in the British zone of Germany, a few miles from the border of the Russian zone, there is a camp for refugees. These refugees or ostfluchtlinge have gone through hardships. Many of them held secret union cards in the Russian zone. The cards were of the dissoluble paper so they could be swallowed in any emergency. They escaped with their lives in their hands.

Max Licht is one of them. He was a champion runner once. Now he has no teeth and looks ridiculous. This does not bother him so much as the attitude of his countrymen.

"We ostfluchtlinge are an inferior race in Germany now," he says. "Nobody likes us or cares much what happens to us. We are outcasts."

Even Germans of two different zones fail to get along. It has been established that World War II could have been shortened by many months and countless lives saved if Allied leaders had been able to overcome their suspicion (or just dislike?) of the German underground, and cooperated with the latter.(Allan Dulles, OSS leader in Switzerland during the war, and Trevor Roper, British historian and former intelligence officer, enumerate the evidence in their books of 1947.)

It is the suspicion *between friends* which has so far prevented a real federation of nations and not "aggressor nations," which, if actually dangerous, form one more argument in favor of federation.

In the same vein, there is a wave of pessimism sweeping the United States now, brought into sharp focus in a series of articles by Manchester Boddy, publisher and editor of the *Los Angeles Daily News*. Usually an intelligent crusader for true progress, Mr. Boddy has in this case become a victim of the fifth revival of Dr. Malthus' gloomy but unfounded predictions about the globe's inability to feed its citizens. Incidentally he proclaims Europe–the whole of Europe–dead and gone! I wish Mr. Manchester Boddy had been with me in Merigny, a little French Village, on Easter Sunday 1949, and had seen the excursion of 150 French children under the direction of their Monsieur Curé. The expressions on the eager little faces, the rallying songs sung with pep, would have convinced him that this surging life did not carry the germ of doom.

In the past half year I have seen 13 newspaper reporters come home from abroad and tell us that people "hate Americans."

I have no doubt that these reporters are truthful in a legal sense. They must have dug up someone, perhaps a black market racketeer, who "hated Americans". But they made no reservations and made no mention of the hundreds and thousands and millions who love and understand Americans. Why?

Because their job was to write a story, something different, and they hoped, perhaps, it would not be taken too seriously. Some years back it was fashionable to write about those who loved America. By and by this was considered trite, and it became the duty of every self-respecting reporter to dig up someone who hated us– however hard he would have to dig.

The reporters have a job to do, but some of them could do it better.

Reporting facts is not always the same as telling the truth.

Even when facts are studied with the best will to get

a complete picture there may still be delusions and grave mistakes because hard facts are given more weight than the possibilities of nations and individuals. The dynamic aspect of life is ignored.

"By isolating a fact in order to study it," wrote Lecomte de Nouy in *The Road to Reason* (Longmans Green, 1949) "we give it a beginning and an end which are artificial and relative. In relation to the evolution of the universe, birth is not a beginning, death is not an end. There are no more isolated phenomena in nature than there are isolated notes in a melody."

Whether as individuals or nations, we are not separate entities. We are not so distant and different from our friends, enemies, and even "aggressor nations" as we are apt to imagine. We are responsible with them for their acts—and able to influence them and solve all our international problems peacefully—if we really want to.

But the means employed to exert influence should be chosen with care, for whatever we do to any nation, to any single man, woman or child, we do it to the Creator or Being who lives and breathes and has his hopes in all.

Chapter 7

Behind Symbols and Dogmas

To believe in dogmas and symbols without understanding their meaning is called superstition. To disbelieve in them without probing their origin is another kind of superstition, which closes the doors of the heart and mind, both to the persons believing in these things and to the knowledge they convey. Such indifference or disbelief is understandable at the present time, however, for the ancient art of writing or reading symbols has been covered with thick layers of dust. Once uncovered, this precious art will appeal as much to modern man as it did to his ancestors thousands of years ago.

There is no end to meanings that can be given to symbols, or read into them. Here will be given some hints of the interpretations of the past, and of the sentiments and ideas inspiring those who created some of the well-known symbols of our ancient traditions, for contemplation and realization.

* * *

The ascent of the Christian era conspicuously brought to the notice of the world the symbol of the cross, which was known from prehistoric times. In spiritual symbolism the vertical line represents the upward, egocentric urge of the individual, which is met by the will or requirements of the community, represented by the horizontal line. This influence appears to hinder or slow down an individual's journey to the goal of his ambitions. As a boy he wants to flee authority and roam the countryside or raid apple orchards or candy stores— while a heartless community of elders requires him to go to school and to curb his greed and limit his enjoyment to the petty proceeds from his parental allowance. First he resents this violently and tries to escape by ruse or war. Later he discovers that the community thus helped him expand his consciousness from his petty self to fellow creatures, enriching his life. As a grown-up he may give of his spare time, wealth, health or comfort for community work and causes. First he feels solemn and awed about this and what he calls his "great sacrifice", but gradually he will realize that he received more than he gave.

If his yearnings be of the rare kind called "spiritual" and he wants to read or meditate in solitude to acquire the wisdom of the ages and the power and contentment of the sages, he may even be called upon to give up such pursuits for the service of his community. He then sacrifices what he calls "spiritual progress" and feels a hero, becoming inflated with the delightful brand of pride which, truthfully, may become a spur to real progress, consuming in its own good time his initial pride. If in addition he is a crusader for some cause not yet generally accepted by his community, such as friendship between different races, soil conservation, a deeper and wider religious outlook or a new and glamorous kind of fertilizer, he is subjected to particular hardships and temptations. The resistance that he feels and the slow pace of progress may stagger him. Seeing most people following what he considers the lesser prophets of the established views or creeds while he is able to gather merely a few followers, perhaps of wavering minds, he may begin to weary and wonder sometimes what station he could have reached, what following he could have obtained, by deviating ever so little from the straight path of his conscience, in order to oblige men and play up to their hunger for sensation.

When, on top of this, even most of his few and simple followers turn away from him— which happens in the life of most men fighting for a cause, he thinks for an agonizing moment that he has been abandoned by both God and man. He thinks he has failed in his efforts and, wondering how even God could let him thus fail, he may exclaim in utter despair, "My God, my God, why hast thou forsaken me!"

That moment of unspeakable suffering is experienced sometime or other by almost every human being who then feels as if not only his physical limbs but also his spiritual hands and feet are nailed, and he is helpless, useless.

So the cross is the symbol of the life of every man, and particularly of that of the pioneer and trailblazer, the vital man.

* * *

In the ancient Hindu traditions there is a philosophical conception of a recurring trinity in the universe: the seer, the seen, and sight—or, God the creator, God the creature and God the process of creation—or God the source of all religion, his son or prophet receiving and interpreting the inspiration, and the inspiration itself, which has been called the Holy Ghost— or again, the prophet and teacher, his followers receiving his teachings and the continuous process of instruction.

The conception of Trinity, therefore, is not any kind of "natural law," nor a dogma which has to be believed, but simply a voluntary classification of mental pictures. The purpose of this classification is merely to clarify these pictures and their mutual relation in our own minds. There are other applications besides the ones mentioned here. The idea is sometimes represented by an equilateral triangle.

* * *

In the ancient Egyptian traditions life was pictured as the waters of the sea. To master the difficulties of life by a philosophical and loving attitude was called "to walk upon the waters," and to calm the mind of oneself and others was called "to still the storm." To sweeten the ordinary life of hard knocks and blows—by a loving and compassionate attitude— was called "to turn the water of life into wine." Sages, poets, teachers, messengers have used to this symbolism right up to the present time. So, in the sacrament of the holy Eucharist, wine is given as a symbol of divine love, which is the lifeblood of the Spirit of Christ, comparable to the flesh of the physical body.

Christ gave up his blood–his love–to heal men's spirit. His loss of actual physical blood on a cross made this symbolism complete and conspicuous and impressed even those who would not so readily have understood or been interested in the subtle and real significance.

By asking his disciples to eat the bread and drink the wine "which is my flesh and blood"–this messenger wanted to avert the attention of his followers from his physical personality to the divine knowledge and the spirit of love, which was his real being, and which is the real being of every man.

This symbolism was also intended to make man realize the unity of the universe, and that even eating and drinking wine is eating the flesh and drinking the blood of God, whose body is this whole universe, including all the good things we eat, and whose blood is the wine of love. The same idea is behind the saying of grace before meals. It is an appreciation of the fact that even what we eat and drink are gifts from the one source, which is God. He feeds us of his body and of his blood–an outpouring of love on all planes of existence. Thus, love is not something abstract, it is not only a feeling, or an inspiration, not even merely an example, but something tangible, including such things as bread and wine and other foods and drinks. It is also steam, electricity and atomic power. It is building our bodies and power plants. It is sustaining our minds and making our hearts tick.

It is in this sense Christ gives his blood that we may be redeemed. This is equally true of all good men and women. They are agents for this outpouring of love, be it in the form of physical gifts or emotional or mental stimulation.

The most spectacular examples are the donors of blood for transfusion to sick fellow-men. They give of their physical blood and of their emotional and mental blood as well, in the form of generous thoughts and good wishes. As these blood donors receive in due time a corresponding amount of blood from the workshop of nature in their own bodies, So do the donors of love, inspiration and generous thoughts receive abundantly from the inexhaustible storehouse of God, and incidentally, much faster than in the physical case.

In this symbolism, then, is hidden the key mystery of our little world: the whole creation is held together and is being run by the vibrations of love. But there is resistance, born of ignorance and laziness, particularly in the world of man, who prides himself on being the prize package of nature. Therefore he is prompted to realize this mystery of love so he can give and receive more abundantly, thus running more smoothly and efficiently his personal life, his business, his community, his recreations, all of which are but foundations for his progress into the worlds of spiritual realization.

Every man is a receiver–and a giver. Every man is the Christ–and a disciple of Christ. The story of Christ is not the story of one particular and peculiar man. It is the story of all men.

Many devoted Christians stand up for the exclusive greatness of Jesus, the man, but this man himself said, "Call me not good– only one is good– that is God"–meaning that his message was not for glorifying one man. It was concerned with the Spirit which embodies all men. The greatness is in the Spirit, not in the individual. This is good news, for the Spirit is always with us. He who has learned to see the greatness of the Spirit directly has his ideal with him everywhere. He may see the Spirit expressed in an individual, as some saw it in Buddha and others saw it in Jesus, and he may see it in nature, in the whole universe–in himself. To a man of such realization it would appear futile, even a sacrilege, to compare different expressions of the Spirit and think of one as greater than the other. If Buddha be the perfect expression of the spirit to some people and Jesus to others, how could one be pronounced greater than the other? How could the Spirit be greater than itself? And who would feel capable of such judgment? Can anyone know the measure of another person without being at least as great, and capable of probing the depths of his heart and mind?

Measuring the greatness of men and comparing them belongs to the world of individuals, a world of limitations. In the world of the Spirit there are no measurements, no comparisons. All are like flutes of reed through which the Spirit plays its music.

* * *

In Hindu mythology, there is an image of an ape, which is called Hanuman. It represents the animal instincts and desires of man. At certain times the priests pour oil on the head of Hanuman. This is a symbolic act meaning that concessions have to be made to the lower part of man. It is meant to remind and impress man with the fact that his nature comprises a primitive, animal part as well as a spiritual one, and that there need be no resentment or sharp contrast between these two parts, but rather a gentle and soothing attitude like the pouring of oil. Passions are as important and natural a part of our being as that which is called Spirit, which may be said to be rooted in the soil of the passions. The Spirit will not be successful, therefore, if trying to root out passions. Its task is to harmonize them with the rest of the personality, and to direct them according to the law of love or, "to show consideration in passion."

That is the goal. Before it has been reached, there may be failures and mistakes—mistakes of judgment, failure of strength. Mistakes of judgment may be just individual. Or they may be expressed in schools of thought temporarily shared by many. But in the long run mistakes do not matter. They are stepping stones to truth and success.

Some complain of having to fight this battle of which they know so little. But how could man become great without having great battles to fight within himself? How could God raise man to his own level if he were to take away from him his free choice and the privilege of making mistakes? Men's experiments and mistakes are God's own experiments and mistakes, carried out through the agency of man. This world is not made yet, it is in the making, unfinished. Man is helping make it and finish it. God is not a teacher in a kindergarten. He is a creator with men as his assistants. He who realizes this will not worry about others—not even about himself. He will look understandingly, compassionately—even admiringly at the heroic efforts of his fellow man and of himself to steer a sound course across the rough sea of life. He will also remember that although the goal in the end be the same, the routes are different. The best course for one is not necessarily good for another. So how could he judge any man? He may even become wary of offering his advice, feeling that a real adviser is always near at hand, whispering directly into the ears of those who want to listen.

* * *

The beautiful symbol of Jesus being born of a virgin and with the Holy Ghost as his father, points to the fact that man is not only a physical being of flesh and blood, but a being of Spirit as well, whose father is the great Spiritual Being in whom we all live and move about and whom we call God and whose spirit we sometimes call the Holy Ghost. Indeed, whenever a woman begets a child, the Spirit of God is upon her and overshadows her, and her very act of giving birth to a child is as much a spiritual process as a physical one. The call of motherhood is sacred.

The mystery of motherhood is a reflection of the creation of the universe—in the world of man. Conception takes place through the merging of two separate individuals into one loving unity. In that moment is born, not only a new individual, but with it a spark of love, which is from then on nursed by the mother and watched with tenderness by the father until it matures into creation. So also, the male and female aspect of God before the dawn of creation merged into one loving power, conceiving a universe to be born. The seed was nurtured by the female aspect and tenderly guarded by the male aspect until the time of maturity and lo—a universe came to life!

As the earth is made fertile by rays of the sun, and as the moon takes its light from the sun and gives out light in its turn, so does woman take into her womb a ray of the spirit with the physical conception, giving it on to the world, in due time, as a soul of a newborn baby.

Says the Gayan by Inayat Khan: "In man God designed his own image, in woman he completed it!"

* * *

In many ancient traditions, the snake has been used as a symbol of the strength, endurance and wisdom required to accomplish great things and particularly to climb the steep path to spiritual attainment. The symbol originated in certain districts of India where there lived, according to ancient legends, large and very powerful snakes of great age.

These snakes were the most independent of all beings. They could live without food for a long time, never complaining or whimpering. When, at long last, they became hungry, they did not have to run along to find their food, but by meditation they made their prey come to them, and finally hypnotized little beasts or birds into running straight into their mouths. They were masters of the jungle and never could be tamed by man or beast. The flame of their minds burned quietly without a flicker and they were content.

The strength, endurance and cunning of a snake are qualities which help one fight any enemy, and particularly the most formidable one: the enemy within—which can be defined as everything which prevents man from becoming the master of his own destiny.

* * *

In all civilizations man has tried to bridge the gap of death with theories of the hereafter, in order to satisfy his urge for continuity, his sense of eternity.

According to one set of teachings, the life hereafter is to be Heaven for the good ones and hell for the bad ones. For simple people of the distant past, or in backward communities of today this teaching may have, or may have had, its value as an inducement to be good. But civilized humanity has now reached a higher morality: man wants to behave for the sake of the community, for its smooth running, and for the sake of friendship, or simply for the sake of behaving. The rude teachings of Heaven or Hell can give place to something closer to reality, although the terms may well be retained.

Heaven may be used as an appropriate term for the state of mind and the condition of happy activity in cooperation with the Creator himself, to which man finally attains after having toiled and fought his way through half-blind selfishness and the feeling of isolation in this life and, eventually, in the immediate hereafter. Heaven may also be used to suggest a temporary state of happiness to which love and pure thoughts and emotions can bring a man even at an early stage of his progress.

As to hell–there is no hell other than that temporary condition or state of mind which man creates for himself or others by immature thoughts, emotions and actions.

In the East, many people adhere to the theory of reincarnation and karma. They think that, with a death of the body, the individual lives on in subtler bodies, shedding one after another until, for a shorter or longer periods, he lives as a very pure and glamorous spiritual being of most aristocratic vibrations. Then, with a bang of guilty conscience like a vacationist who feels the call of duty, he starts along the downward path again, putting on bodies of progressively coarser matter until finally, he is reborn as a wide-eyed baby on earth. His parents, surroundings and conditions are supposed to have been chosen by his own soul in accordance with its actions, thoughts and emotions in earlier lives–so no complaints allowed!

To many people this bright idea has given comfort and proud satisfaction. It is natural and sometimes desirable to adopt, at a certain stage, a theory of life which will appear logical and satisfy one's craving for justice. Many have the good sense to consider their theories–just theories. Others take them literally, priding themselves on knowing. This very pride and deception may bar them from real knowledge if and when such opportunity is offered. The condition of the next world cannot be embodied in any theory or written statement and cannot be studied in any book. It cannot even remotely be portrayed by a language concerned exclusively with the things of this world. Mountain climbers often find it difficult to give expression to the exclusive views and sceneries they enjoy from the peaks they conquer. Aviators know it to be almost impossible to portray by word pictures the weird, magnificent world unfolded before their wondering eyes at high altitudes. How futile, then, trying to explain a world that cannot be seen with the eyes we have and know here, but only with a different pair of eyes of which as little is known as about that other world!

For those who feel that the theory of reincarnation gives the only logical explanation of certain facts, another explanation will be offered not as a rival theory but merely in the hope of loosening the grip of a dogma upon certain minds.

In ancient Egyptian and Hindu traditions the physical existence of man was called a shadow of the shadow or an imprint upon an imprint. The meaning was that the original and most real existence of man, his soul, which was called a ray of God, has produced an imprint on a denser matter and this imprint has produced another imprint upon a still denser matter and so on down the line until we come to the last and densest imprint, which was the physical existence. The number of successive imprints were considered more or less a matter of choice, like the number of colors in the rainbow, which is really infinite but which can be limited to a definite number for all practical purposes.

This "imprinting" was considered to be going on simultaneously and forever on all planes of existence. When viewed by humans in the physical existence, as we do now, the illusion of "time" enters in, an illusion limited to the physical and neighboring spheres and born from these spheres. Even observers who are called clairvoyant, who are able to perceive things beyond the scope of the known physical senses will usually interpret what they "see" according to the limitations of the physical existence, as long as their minds function in this existence. To such observers, therefore, it will appear as if the soul to be born on earth carries with it as "bodies" these imprints which have been made upon denser and denser matters, and this appears to happen in successive stages of time.

These matters upon which imprints have been made are the same matters which appear to have been "discarded" by "returning" souls, coming "from" the earth. Suppose that the observer watches a soul with a musical inclination "approaching" earth, and it "meets the soul of Beethoven, returning." The oncoming soul becomes deeply impressed with the musical substance matter which Beethoven "discards," and Beethoven, on his side, is glad to impress the oncoming soul with his achievements. The soul on its way to earth "brings with it" the music of Beethoven, plays it, lives it, thinks it. Now, if the observer cannot distinguish the real soul of Beethoven, but just his music, his thoughts, emotions, characteristics, he will say that the oncoming soul is Beethoven reincarnated! And the assertion will not be without some truth. Only he whose observation can penetrate to the very soul will know that the newcomer is not Beethoven himself. He may be called his pupil, or simply his music.

All the facts which some people have counted as proofs of the ordinary theory of reincarnation can be easily explained by this second theory. For lovers of metaphysics many more theories could be given. But he who would know the truth, let him turn his thoughts away, for a while, from all speculations, from any bustling activity and keep his mind like the still water of a lake, in which reality may be reflected.

* * *

The term karma refers to the fate a person is supposed to have brought upon himself by his actions, words, thoughts or emotions all through the many lives he is believed to have lived from the beginning of man's existence on earth. The corresponding law of the science of physics is the law of cause and effect. To most of those who adhere to the theory of reincarnation, everything that happens to a human being is considered a result of his or her own previous acts, thoughts or emotions. This conception gives relief from the heartbreak a sensitive person may go through by seeing the sufferings of others. But is such a relief good for man or helpful for humanity? It has often been observed to cool the ardor with which man goes to help his fellow and reform his community. He may still help but with an ungenerous and irrelevant side thought that, after all, the people who suffer have in some way deserved it. Indeed, this point of view is known to have degraded whole nations. If the point of view was strictly true, however, this could not be helped but if the theory of reincarnation be not correct, neither will the corresponding theory of karma be accurate. If man does not revisit this present existence life after life, how can he have accumulated causes to form and mold his present life? The solution may be found by following the old advice of forgetting one's petty self for a moment and turning the attention to the group, to humanity. Even if there will always be a law of cause and effect it need not be pinned to the individual. It may be understood in a larger sense.

A shipyard may turn out very seaworthy crafts in a minimum of time and be considered the pride of the nation even though a few workers be inefficient. The more able workers and designers make up for the less able so that the whole result becomes commendable. This may go on without the inefficient ones even knowing that they are not up to scratch. Now, to use an expression from another field of human endeavor: the able workers carry the burden for the others and "atone for their sins." The semblance maybe carried a step further. An experienced craftsman may take the inefficient workers through a training course, thus raising them to a respectable level and "saving" them. Even in a football or baseball game a team may do pretty well in spite of one or a few poor players, although in this case, with the critical public armed with soft tomatoes, spoiled eggs and empty Coca-Cola bottles, the poor unsuccessful players may not be in a position to remain oblivious of their plight.

As the shipyard and the football ground are nothing but true reflections of the Spirit world, the laws and rules are exactly the same. The group as a whole, or humanity as a whole, has to reap the consequences of its accumulated actions. But each single individual has a certain leeway. He may carry less than his own burden or more—within any considered period of time. What happens in the course of eternity is another matter, which could be considered only by minds geared to eternity.

So, while there is a law of karma, applying for all practical purposes to the group only, there is a law of grace applying to the individual, preventing good or spiritual men or women to take upon themselves greater burdens than their own individual debts. This is "atonement." This is the meaning of Christ taking our sins upon his shoulders. Not only Christ does this but any good man or woman. There is a curious idea with many sincere people that this is unjust. Of course, anyone is within his rights to fight, with fist or mind, against anything he considers unjust, even if it be the rules and bylaws according to which this universe is being run by its perpetual Creator. Another approach to the cause of justice may be to investigate the basis for one's own conception thereof.

* * *

The man for whom that his burden is thus relieved, in accordance with the law of grace, can also do his bit. The clumsy worker in the shipyard may take one of two attitudes. He may be a bully or a malcontent to counteract his feeling of inferiority, thus making it hard for the others to cover up his deficiency and make good his mistakes. Or he may humbly regret his shortcomings and ask for their help, which will smoothen things and ensure a better results from the assistance offered him. In the world of the Spirit this attitude is known as "repentance" and is expressed through *prayer*. It is said that "when ardent prayer rises from the heart" the response will come. This is not because God or saints or good people need to be asked before they will help, but because prayer tunes the mind and heart, preparing the recipient to benefit from what he will receive.

But prayer is not merely or even mainly the asking favors. Saints and sages live their lives in constant prayer although they think of nothing but giving. Prayer is tuning mind and heart to the vibrations of the spirit. Prayer is leading one's thoughts and emotions along a certain path. Then one may wish to stop at choice spots of beauty and take in the view. This is called contemplation or meditation. Both processes lift mind and heart above the daily chores, worries, fears or grudges and make one receptive to inspiration.

Prayer or contemplation does not affect only him who prays, but spreads throughout the universe as vibrations, like all other mental or emotional activities, affecting with different strength all other minds and hearts. So even those who pray in the solitude of monasteries or mountain caves do influence others. But this influence does not always come up to expectations and is not usually a good enough excuse for running away from the world. Often the urge to run away and hide stems from fear or oversensitivity and should be fought. Therefore the Lord's advice to Arjuna in the *Bhagavad-Gita* is to retain his prayerful attitude and his sobriety of mind and heart–while going back into the battle and fighting! Life in this world, with its responsibilities, wars, and worries and jarring influences was thus made for man and particularly for his spiritual awakening and evolution and is not to be shunned by him who wants to grow and know. There is no progress for him in leaving this for the luxury of solitude, except for occasional refreshments. Progress is expressed in his attitude.

There is no sweeter fragrance than of prayers rising from the workbench or the din of battle.

Chapter 8

A Road and a Path

This is an allegory retold in every religious tradition and particularly in mystic lore, the core of wisdom common to all religions. The aim is to describe and to map a landscape of mind and spirit by means of similes taken from the physical world. This is the world in which our senses function and it is believed to be nothing but "frozen thoughts"—a crystallization of mind and spirit. But there are differences between water and ice and so also between spirit and matter.

If the community of thoughtful herring had been frozen in ice too long to remember the gay life in liquid water, such herring would look with icy skepticism and suspicion at anyone trying to tell them about the unheard of mobility, variability and capriciousness of that water world. Similarly, it takes some effort for the earthbound to realize the mobility and shiftiness of the fairy world of the Spirit. Its subtler and quicker vibrations make a mockery of "time" and "space" as we know these formidable monsters, and makes it seem as if anything that ever happens there continues to happen all the time, everywhere.

Thus prepared and forewarned, we may now polish up Aladdin's lamp and see if its ancient spirit will not also do the bidding of modern man.

There is a main road of life (so the story goes), wide and of gentle ascent, along which man may travel as far as he likes, at whatever speed he prefers. The road passes through gardens of rare beauty and sweet scents and also through barren deserts. It leads through moments of happiness and hours of suffering. It does not treat all men alike. Some travel at ease while others seem to meet nothing but hardships. But such hardships maybe found in the end to have benefited the traveler more than the easy flow of pleasure.

Many follow this road for a long time, some even to the end. Others are anxious to find a path and make a shortcut. They are yearning to know, not only physical facts, but also the deeper sense and meaning of life. If they want this knowledge in order to qualify and better serve their fellow man, then, says the story, they will discover in due time that there *is* such a path. It may be entered at any point along the road. But it looks steep and forbidding to any wanderer who is not burning with the fever of love!

Both the road and the path lead to the same final goal, which may be called heaven. But there is a difference in time and in the attitude. The path is shorter and implies a conscious effort to reach one's destination. One travels with one's face to the goal. On the road one is sometimes pulled along with one's back to the goal, which one does not see, since one does not look for it.

People may not always know whether they are on the road or the path. There are no physical distinctions to go by. Ardent servants of religion may be among the bold climbers of the path, if they chose this course for love of truth and man. But no membership of any institution does of itself lead thither. On the other hand, many who never embraced or understood religion are following the path of service by virtue of their actions and their attitude.

The advice given in religious scriptures to a climber on the path maybe very different from that given to a wanderer along the road. Unless the dual teachings of the road and the path be realized, the scriptures will therefore appear contradictory. But the wanderer on the road rarely cares. Before him is the wide, white ribbon of a road, so long that it seems to reach right into eternity, so broad and accommodating there appears to be no reason for leaving it. It is thronged with people, some gay, laughing, insouciant, some sad, some running, some dancing, some just walking soberly. They are having one long, good party. They are actors in a great play. Why should they even remember that there is a steep and tiresome path leading up from that road? What do they care if the scriptures seem contradictory? This may even appear to them an attractive excuse for ignoring Religion's challenging appeal!

But here and there along with wide white ribbon one notices a figure creep silently away—or march boldly along—toward the prickly hedge which lines the road, and gradually emerge to climb the narrow path which winds like a piece of twisted string up the side of the mountain. It is of such an ardent climber it may be demanded that he put forth his left cheek when struck on the right. This does not concern the carefree wanderer on the road. But to the latter applies the challenge to defend his right: "all they that take the sword shall perish by the sword!" This is not only a warning to aggressors but also an encouragement to resist them. Who would there be to let an insolent attacker perish by the sword if everyone were busy offering the other cheek?

To all appearances, climbers on the path, too, travel in gay company, yet, for them each course is different. While serving his companions, each wanderer will also find himself alone, in quest of unmapped land, sometimes facing no harder obstacles than nettles and thorns, but often threatened by ferocious beasts of prey. Also, his trail may become so narrow that he will have to leave behind him all his possessions to be able to go on ahead. He will hear the challenging call, "If thou wilt be perfect go and sell what thou hast and give to the poor, and thou shalt have treasure in heaven; and come and follow me." But such is not the message to humanity at-large; at any rate not for a long time to come. "If thou wilt be perfect…" is the clue to the climbers on the path.

The perfection they seek is not the same kind as that of a great scientist, artist, writer or statesman. The climber on the path would like to reach such perfection too, but he cannot help putting it second to his primary aim: the perfection of sentiment and character. To achieve this takes the better part of his strength and talent. Since his ticket of admission to the path was not worldly accomplishment but simply an urge to serve rather than enjoy, he may have entered as a very simple soul. His ascent may not have improved upon his worldly treasures of mind. To many, he may appear crude and unevolved, if his particular approach be not understood. On the other hand, great scientists, artists, writers, statesmen may be generous, conscientious, inspired and doing most important work, yet know nothing of this particular "path of service" which may be beyond their interest and imagination. But when, occasionally, such a giant of the road does understand, and chooses the hardships of the path, his spirit soars, passing millions who entered long before him, and he becomes a masterful servant, bridging heaven and earth.

The wanderers on the road and on the path combine to carry the ship of humanity to its destination. There could therefore be no more preference for one or the other then there would be for deckhands or stokers on a steamer. As far as importance goes, they are equals. This is rarely realized by either. The present need is not so much conversion from one to the other, but realization of the nature and true unity of both.

Moral codes, rules of behavior, ideals and ideas, while inwardly alike, may outwardly appear different, sometimes directly opposite for the wanderers on the road and climbers of the path. While the first will rightly seek position, wealth and fame, the latter may sometimes seek poverty, though this is no final end. It merely helps them understand the conditions of the poor, while they later may seek to experience the sentiments of the rich, thus treasuring the genuine qualities of both while rising above their limitations. While people on the road rightly "honor their father and mother that they may live long and prosper in their country," the climbers on the path may sometimes be called upon to turn their backs upon father and mother and friends for the sake of their ideal—in which they see the real, deeper being of their father, mother, friends. Whereas it is good for most people on the road to acquire a certain uniformity and stability of life, habits, creed and ideas, the climbers on the path may frequently feel the urge of changing. Since convictions mean more to them than tradition, reputation or peace, they will follow the promptings of their hearts rather than of their neighbors, and may seem to spend much of their time enthusiastically acquiring dogmas and beliefs—and as enthusiastically discarding them. During such changes and because of them, the ardent climber may be the target of withering comment by acquaintances of itchy tempers, which may help him acquire the blessed immunity of a generous heart.

Often he does not contend himself with changing beliefs. He may also frequently change his line of work, or even pursue a number of activities at the same time, drawing acid remarks from his more stable-minded compatriots who are sticking to their groove with steadfast stubbornness. However, if we follow the jumpings-around of this eager climber, we may find coherence in his jumping. We may find he touched as with a magic wand the various fields into which he barged, apparently so unprepared. He may be an executive with a great number of companies at his fingertips. He may be an organizational giant in the social or religious field. What gives him this touch of success in so many spheres, and what gives him the itch to cover them all? The path he is climbing is that of life as a whole. He is seeking the essentials, applying to all fields of endeavor. His urge is to discover the vital elements of life and make them work in as many different spheres and activities as he can cover. Based on the knowledge of such vital elements, he gains an insight into all activities at once, which another may acquire in his special field only after a lifetime of plodding work and study. This does not mean that the climber of the path will master the details of such various fields as well as the experts, but he may have visions which only exceptional experts can share.

In his friendships the climber on the path maybe as exuberant as in his beliefs and occupations. He never changes friends, for he cannot stop loving those who he already knows, but there is no end to new acquisitions. This, again, may be the cause of both acrid and hilarious verbiage on the part of the more plodding acquaintances who may deem superficial or insincere such capacity and haste in making friends. But the climber on the path is not superficial. His very prompting is that love which penetrates with painful insistence to the depth of things and beings. Upon whomever such love shines, it uncovers secrets, draws forth response. A casual glance from a passerby on the street may make such a lover of men ponder and suffer for days, because of the tragedy he saw revealed in that single flash. A handshake may mean more to him and give him greater confidence than a signed contract. This does not mean that he reads other peoples minds—he becomes part of them, without any desire or effort to do so. He does not know the tedious details, but he feels deeply the general condition. This is both exhilarating and painful. All their joys are his, as well as their sorrows. And as he feels with their hearts and in a general way, sees with their minds, so his initial love is magnified to a surging sense of oneness, and he must love them with the same desperate intensity with which every being loves himself. Although real love is always a blessing, this increased capacity may cause unfounded expectations or irregularities of behavior that may offend less fiery members of the community. This is an explanation, not an excuse, for any ardent climber who may occasionally fail in his judgment or lose the balance of mind which should be his first and also last concern. Usually, however, such mistakes do not happen to a genuine climber on the path, but rather to immature adventurers who frivolously gamble with their mental or emotional gifts and talents.

Those who hunt for unusual powers or experiences may pursue this hunt to their hearts' desire, but let them not confuse such quest with the ardent path of service, whose wanderers are prompted by love in which all self-seeking must drown. To these, too, power will come— the power of love.

Nevertheless, among the seekers for sensation there are many prospective climbers on the path. They may have the wrong emphasis, temporarily. They may pay homage and shower their exquisite loyalty upon high priests who are not deserving. But through the side road they will gain experience and may find their bearings, emerging, eventually, upon the genuine path of service. They too will leave behind them the companions who are still too deeply entrenched in their conceit to hear the voices of their hearts. But the latter too, may come along in due time—drawn by the love of those who went ahead. Eventually all the friends of climber on the path will be carried to their final destination by that very love which they considered superficial or insincere because it could not always materialize into the earthly ties. Then they, too, will realize that genuine love is beyond all ties, unlimited, all-comprising. For the benefit of those who do not yet know or feel this, a wise man of yore said "judge not, lest you be judged." For him who has love, this advice is not needed. He cannot judge.

As human curiosity was the cause and basis of science and many other distinguished fields of endeavor, so also on the path curiosity is the driving force. In the beginning it may express itself in beliefs and theories about life and death, about earth and heaven. As the climber begins to realize that theories and beliefs may become obstacles rather than means to true revelation, he discards them. There are things which cannot be expressed in the language of this world any more than music could be explained to one who could not hear. But things that cannot be spoken may be sensed or felt and, as the climber advances in this art, he will be distinguished by a habit of taking a farsighted view of things. His interest will be in matters of lasting importance and he will not worry about trifles or momentary losses. He will think and dream in terms of communities, nations, humanity—yet, without ever running out of affection for his individual friends. But the latter may become mildly desperate in the face of his gay indifference to their daily worries and his ferocious interest in the development of their souls! They may feel however, that even his indifference is not caused by lack of understanding but by a deeper than usual understanding. So his friend or wife or husband or child may forgive and even enjoy his indifference as much as they treasure his genuine affection.

Only the boldest can pass through the *needle's eye* on the path. At this point they are called upon to give up and lose their very identity—as they know it—in order to merge into their chosen ideal. Whether by the hand of a friend and teacher, or alone, they jump into the darkness, not knowing where they will land, or if they will land. Such is their choice. Doubts and fears may then tower up before them, and they may even lose their foothold and tumble all the way down to the road, which they may then follow for a while to start anew on the path at a later time.

When the climber has passed the needle's eye (so the story ends) he discovers that, far from losing himself by that fateful jump, he found a dazzling world which, from now on, he may call himself. What he once considered self-sacrifice and supreme renunciation now appears to have been but the beginning of his reign as King. From then on there is no turning back, only continuous contemplation of views and vistas that hold him spellbound. For this wanderer there are no more tedious trials, no more weariness. He moves even faster towards that moment when, it has been said, the trees in the forest, the fish in the sea, the beasts of the earth and all human beings will be enlivened by a surging ecstasy without yet knowing why: the universe is celebrating the rebirth of a soul, merging into Life Eternal.

CHAPTER 9

THE CARAVAN GOES ON

Once upon a time, in the old romantic days, it was an Eastern king who ruled with an iron hand his subjects, of whom some enjoyed a limited liberty, while others were abject slaves. A modern man would shudder at such social conditions— except if he happened to contemplate millions of modern slave workers, who have less hope, or certain modern rulers who have no less power than the ancient Kings but lack their grace.

In the palace of this ancient Eastern ruler one of the humblest slaves attracted the attention of the king, because of his conscientious work and good behavior–which ruler of today has ever shown that much concern for his modern slave workers?–So the king set free that slave and made him a clerk in one of his departments. The former slave worked so faithfully and showed such talents that the king raised him to even higher positions until, at long last, he made him his treasurer and most trusted minister. But this was much resented by the people of distinction at the court who, every one of them, had secretly coveted this position. All the time they had looked with concern at the meteoric rise of the former slave. Now they intimated to the king that such a man could not be trusted, and that in such a responsible position he would certainly be on the lookout for an opportunity to enrich himself. The king decided to be advised by them. They kept a vigilant eye on the new treasurer, however, hoping to catch him at some sinister and dishonest act.

One day they thought they had succeeded. One of the ministers approached the king and told him that, at last, they had proof that the new treasurer was a common thief. They had spied on him and found that on several successive nights, at midnight, the former slave locked himself into the treasury, carrying with him a bag. He locked the door behind him and remained inside for quite a while, finally to emerge with his bag and then very quietly retreat to his quarters. Now, what would the treasurer do alone in the treasury at midnight except carry with him in his bag some of the treasures?

The king became very sad and promised to investigate the matter. The following day he hid himself near the door of the treasury and, as his informant had said,, at midnight the former slave arrived with his bag and locked himself in. The king, having a key of his own, walked in after him quietly, so that he was not discovered.

In the treasury the former slave opened his bag and took out a bundle of dirty, ragged clothes. He took off the resplendent uniform he had been wearing as a treasurer and put on the old rags. He then stood up before a great mirror, bowed into his own image and said, "Greetings to you, slave. This is what you were before the king by his grace raised you to your present position. May you never forget it! May you never succumb to the illusion of pride, but always serve faithfully your king and master to whom you owe your life and everything you possess!"

The King rose from his hiding place and came forward and embraced the faithful servant, saying that henceforth he was not only his trusted minister but also his friend and teacher, having taught him by his example the relation of any man to that King and Creator to whom we owe everything we possess and our very lives.

To one who has felt the lure of the East this story may bring to life visions of caravans in the desert. He may imagine that he hears again gentle thuds of camel hoofs in soft sand dunes and sees rhythmic movements of graceful animals, unhurried, dignified, whether under a scorching noontime sun or when night falls, the riders having lit their torches and the flickering flames darting up and down with the even strides of the desert ships. Every rider knows that his life and his fate are irrevocably linked to the others for the duration of the journey. Alone he would perish. He depends on the whole caravan for water, food, protection against robbers. Also, he is proud to know that he is one of the team on which all depend. Humility and pride, sympathy and devotion to the common goal unite them in an indivisible brotherhood of achievement.

Similarly, every rider across the desert and through the gardens of life may look ahead— and back, deriving assurance, pride and humility from the vision of the caravan of humanity. Like the slave and his kingly friend, he will realize that his possessions, conditions, thoughts and emotions can be traced to unending numbers of fellow riders right down from the distant past. He may have boasted of being "self-made" in a rash moment but now he remembers that even his body and mind were handed to him by agencies of which he knows little. His nourishment is being prepared by a host of busy workers in bodies of animals and plants, finally to be made palatable by fellow humans in factories and kitchens.

The thoughtful rider may add some gloomy meditations to his prayers of thanks. Like a camel rising after a rest, grumbling, twisting its nose with exasperation at the rider's prodding stick, its back aching under the heavy load, so many a human rider in the caravan of humanity may grumble because he feels he is carrying a heavier responsibility than he cares to or, more often, because his burden is too trivial. This is the greater hardship. Youngsters yearning to pitch in with all they have for the good of their communities may find red tape, rules, regulations, "lack of funds" and other queer and lame excuses barring them from ample expression of their talents, leaving some entirely without jobs! Such things happen only when the community or its leaders forget the simple pattern of the caravan and the close dependence between the riders, of whom every one is raring to serve the caravan—before he is rebuffed. As the leader of the desert caravan counts all the little flickering lights when night falls, to see that every rider with his torch is with him, so it was assured in the ancient books that not a sparrow falls to the ground without the knowledge of the Father who art in Heaven. Thus, in the world of the Spirit, on which the caravan of humanity is patterned, none is left behind. There is a unique and ample part to be played by every single man, woman and child. This, then, is the goal toward which the caravan of humanity is inevitably moving and which will set free the slaves.

A slave however, is not only one who is imprisoned or mistreated by his community but also one who is chained by the fetters of his own limitations, passions and grudges. A free man is one who has broken these fetters and whose passions have become the servants of his spirit. A slave may become free in a moment's time if he has by his side a kingly soul who looks through his ragged clothes and the dirt on his face to the inner greatness. Every man is looking for such kingly souls among the riders near him, who will not pounce upon him with accusations or drown him in quagmires of gossip, who will not seize his soul in its flights and nail it to evil, delaying the entire caravan—who, rather, will help him discover and express the dazzling light of his spirit, making him jubilantly free and hastening the pace toward freedom for all humanity.

A perfectly healthy boy, complaining about stomach ache after the traditional raid on the apple orchard, may be told "there is always something the matter with that tummy of yours"—and so have stomach trouble all the rest of his life, thanks to this kind suggestion. A young brave, having ventured into the turbulent stream of marriage, may forgetfully be shouting exuberant bachelor nicknames after his shirt stud, disappearing playfully under the chest of drawers one morning—only to be told by his new master and pacesetter that he has a "temper." This pronouncement may actually supply him with one—for life.

Companions with genuine power of observation see only the flaming torch of the soul and its great destination, ignoring with generous smiles the little spots of premature actions or sentiments. They know the caravan has yet a long way to travel. Instead of delaying the pace they are eager to hasten it and make the journey pleasant and refreshing. To those who are submerged in despair and disappointments, seeing nothing but injustice and suffering, they whisper gentle encouragement, pointing to that future when the sufferer's dreams of better worlds will have become blazing realities while the present grim reality will be but a bleak dream of the past. They strengthen the faith of the weary pioneer by reminding him that no effort is ever wasted, that the world as it is today is a passing show of no endurance while the lasting and real thing is the process of creation always going on, in which everyone takes part, consciously or through the fragrance of personality and convictions.

At the present time the writer is looking around with furtive glances. He has rubbed his lamp and aroused a monster. He is wondering whether this gaudy thing will serve or break him. He is not sure whether to be proud or ashamed of it. But, discreetly covering His face, the leader of the Caravan is smiling. Utilizing the inventiveness and drive of man, His progeny, He has presented him with this new gadget, like a father who hands his son a sharp axe, at the proper age, to teach him craftsmanship and care. He has set the stage and has us cornered. By this subtle gift, man is being forced to wise and cooperative action or to the spiritual achievement intended for him by the Master Playwright.

Pausing awhile and looking at the show from the point of view of the Playwright, the writer will see that his present predicament is just one scene of a drama with many acts yet to come. His fear will vanish and a quiet chuckle warm his heart. Then he will again be serious, not from fear but because he realizes the urgency of the play and of keeping to schedule so the acts to come may unfold on time. He has seen the only reality in a world of many claims and pretences. He would not want to delay the onward march of the Caravan of Love.

Acknowledgements

This authorized edition of *Man and This Mysterious Universe* has been published as it was originally written by Brynjolf Björset.

His original acknowledgement read:

It would be impractical to enumerate the books, manuscripts, oral traditions, personal talks and other sources upon which the author has drawn, but he wishes to thank, particularly, Dr. James Jeans, Dr. Chandra Bose, Dr. Oscar Brunler, Dr. Philip Boswood Ballard, Dr Robert A. Millikan and Dr. Grace Watson. The latter three have seen the script in various stages and by their criticism contributed to the final work for which, however, they are not responsible. The book was inspired by the late Inayat Khan, musician and modern sage.

Man and this Mysterious Universe is a publication of the Shamcher Archives, dedicated to preserving and publishing the works of Shamcher Bryn Beorse. It was previously published in 1949 by Philosophical Library, NY.

We are grateful to Diane Feught for her insightful cover design and to Joe Clare, patron of the arts and humanity, for his support for the production of this edition.

Find background to the book, reference links, and further details at:

www.mysterious-universe.shamcher.com

About the Author

Born in Norway in 1896, Brynjolf Björset later emigrated to the US, shortening his name to Bryn Beorse (1896-1980). He authored many non-fiction books, novels and articles, covering topics of energy, economics, full employment, and global awareness as well as Yoga and Sufism.

He worked and travelled in over 65 countries in his lifetime. Fluent in several languages, his comprehensive worldview included the inner meditative life as well as the accomplishment of life in the world. Sent on a UN economic mission to Tunisia in the 1960's, helping to rebuild the Norwegian economy after WWII, Beorse also spent time in exploration, travelling to the Kumbha Mela in India, living in the dunes of Oceano, and going to China at the time of the revolution. A spy in WWII, he was part of the plot to kidnap Hitler. An advocate of the giro-credit economic system, he spoke out against the stagnation of hierarchical organization.

An accomplished Yogi and Sufi, (known as Shamcher) he was instrumental in developing Sufi centres throughout the world, in the tradition of Inayat Khan. He dedicated the last years of his life to OTEC, Ocean Thermal Energy Conversion, a source of benign solar power from the sea. He passed away in Berkeley, California in 1980.

More info at: www.shamcher.org

www.ingramcontent.com/pod-product-compliance
Lightning Source LLC
Chambersburg PA
CBHW070952180426
43194CB00042B/2347